Rodgers & Hammerstein's

CAROUSEL

The Applause Libretto Library Series

Rodgers & Hammerstein's

CAROUSEL

*The Complete Book and Lyrics
of the Broadway Musical*

Music by Richard Rodgers
Book and Lyrics by Oscar Hammerstein II
Based on the play *Liliom* by Ferenc Molnár
(As adapted by Benjamin Glazer)

APPLAUSE
THEATRE & CINEMA BOOKS

AN IMPRINT OF HAL LEONARD LLC

Published in 2016 by Applause Theatre & Cinema Books
An Imprint of Hal Leonard LLC
7777 West Bluemound Road
Milwaukee, WI 53213

Trade Book Division Editorial Offices
33 Plymouth St., Montclair, NJ 07042

Printed in the United States of America

Book compositor: UB Communications

Library of Congress Cataloging-in-Publication Data

Names: Hammerstein, Oscar, II, 1895-1960, author. | Libretto for (work):
  Rodgers, Richard, 1902-1979. Carousel. | Libretto based on (work):
  Molnár, Ferenc, 1878-1952. Liliom.
Title: Carousel : the complete book and lyrics of the Broadway musical /
  music by Richard Rodgers ; book and lyrics by Oscar Hammerstein II ; based
  on the play Liliom by Ferenc Molnár.
Description: Montclair : Applause Theatre & Cinema Books, 2016.
Identifiers: LCCN 2016014486 | ISBN 9781495056581 (pbk.)
Subjects: LCSH: Musicals—Librettos.
Classification: LCC ML50.R67 C3 2016 | DDC 782.1/40268—dc23
LC record available at https://lccn.loc.gov/2016014486

ISBN 978-1-4950-5658-1

www.applausebooks.com

To Gemze de Lappe and Bruce Pomahac
Keepers of the Flame

CONTENTS

INTRODUCTION

In Richard Rodgers's autobiography, *Musical Stages*, he wrote: "One of the most frequent questions I am asked is: 'What is your favorite of all your musicals?' My answer is *Carousel*. Oscar never wrote more meaningful or more moving lyrics, and to me, my score is more satisfying than any I've ever written . . . it affects me deeply every time I see it performed." In 1999, in its "Best of the Century" list, *Time* magazine named *Carousel* the Best Musical of the 20th century, writing that "Rodgers and Hammerstein set the standards for the 20th century musical, and this show features their most beautiful score and the most skillful and affecting example of their musical storytelling." High praise indeed.

Carousel was placed in that impossible position: the follow-up to the historic and surprising success of the first collaboration between composer Richard Rodgers and lyricist/librettist Oscar Hammerstein II. *Oklahoma!* broke new ground when it opened in 1943, and when asked what Rodgers should do as a follow-up, Hollywood's Samuel Goldwyn famously said, "Shoot yourself!" The impact was that strong. Since the two gentlemen realized that working together was clearly successful, both artistically and financially, there was every reason to sit down and come up with another musical. They just needed to find an idea. In their previous careers, they had each created shows on subjects as diverse as the son of the Grand Chinese Eunuch wanting to escape from following in his father's footsteps (Rodgers's *Chee-Chee*) and an English girl captured by an African tribe that thinks she is a princess, who then falls in love with a visiting German named Steve Allen, with whom she escapes (Hammerstein's *Golden Dawn*). So pretty much any story was ripe for musicalization in these creative hands.

It was the people who ran the Theater Guild and brought the team together, Theresa Helburn and Lawrence Langner, who suggested an adaptation of Hungarian writer Ferenc Molnár's *Liliom*. Both Rodgers and Hammerstein rejected it instantly—they had planted their flag with an American story, and they didn't like the idea of going to Hungary. "Why not change the locale to someplace in America?" Helburn and Langner asked. The first idea was New Orleans—because of all the European influences felt in that Creole town, there could be cultural references aplenty. But Hammerstein was skeptical. (He had had an unfortunate experience with *Sunny River* a few years earlier, also set in New Orleans.) Rodgers then suggested the coast of Maine—with the rugged New Englanders taking over for the tough characters that Molnár had created. That idea stuck.

And so began the journey to *Carousel*. Many of the same creative team signed on again, most notably choreographer Agnes de Mille. Her dances, including perhaps the mother of all "dream ballets," helped define the new way of thinking of how important choreography could be in a musical. In the "If I Loved You" sequence, the "conditional love song" was taken to a height that has never been equaled. And the prologue, "The Carousel Waltz," created something entirely new, neither an overture nor a dance but a pantomimic prelude to the story that followed.

Stephen Sondheim has remarked that "*Oklahoma!* is about a picnic; *Carousel* is about life and death." Its themes are big, its characters are rich, its poetry is profound, and its music is deeply emotional. But there is also a problem: central to the story is the fact that the leading man, Billy Bigelow, hits his wife. Yes, he defends his actions by explaining that he and his wife, Julie, had an argument, which he lost, and so he hit her—but he also (in the final version of the script, it should be noted) claimed to have hit her only once—and can't understand why it seems like such a big deal with everyone. To audiences, though, he is a wife beater, an abuser. And that has proven to be a problem that modern productions have to deal with. One way to look at it is that he pays dearly for his actions—mistakes can't simply be brushed aside. And there are those, like Billy Bigelow, who keep resisting admitting personal failures. He makes the same mistake when allowed to come back from heaven for a day, even though he has changed his conditional "if I loved you" into the un-equivocal "you will never know how I loved you." But it's far too late—what's happened has happened.

That said, *Carousel* is arguably the most dramatic of all the Rodgers and Hammerstein shows. In my early days at the office, I saw a production done by one of Manhattan's amateur theatrical troupes, the St. Barts Players, housed in the parish house of St. Bartholomew's Church on Park Avenue and 50th Street. While I watched the earnest production, I was struck by its drama and felt it to be the most logical candidate for some new production that could begin a renewed appreciation of the works of Rodgers and Hammerstein. We were still in the land of Yul Brynner, when the thinking was that for Broadway, these properties could only be star vehicles. Something about *Carousel* made me feel the world of *A Chorus Line*, *Les Misérables*, and *The Phantom of the Opera* would be receptive to the dramatic depths and just plain quality of *Carousel*.

Luckily, my thoughts corresponded with those of Cameron Mackintosh, who was contemplating providing funding for pro-ductions of musicals at the Royal National Theatre in London. *Carousel* was the show that he focused on as the first, and together with the people at the National, he assembled the creative team, headed by director Nicholas Hytner and designer Bob Crowley.

That production opened in London in December 1992 and made its way to Lincoln Center Theater two years later, winning all five Tony Awards for which it was nominated, including the first one (of six so far) for Audra McDonald, who played Carrie. It was what I had hoped for, and it began a global reassessment of the Rodgers and Hammerstein canon.

Today, *Carousel* is attractive to opera companies and symphony orchestras in addition to traditional theaters. Lyric Opera of Chicago presented a well-received production in 2015 with Steven Pasquale and Laura Osnes leading a stellar cast, directed and choreographed by Rob Ashford and imaginatively designed by Paolo Ventura. The New York Philharmonic presented a first-rate concert version in 2013 that was filmed for *Live from Lincoln Center*, directed by John Rando, choreographed by Warren Carlyle, and conducted by Rob Fisher, with a crossover cast that included Nathan Gunn, Kelli O'Hara, Tiler Peck, Robert Fairchild, and Stephanie Blythe. As I write this, plans are afoot for a new production that could prove to be as exciting for today's audiences as Nicholas Hytner's was twenty-five years ago.

Walk on . . . walk on . . . with hope in your heart.

Ted Chapin
The Rodgers & Hammerstein Organization

CAROUSEL

The Applause Libretto Library Series

A note on the dialect: Through his libretto and lyrics to *Carousel*, Oscar Hammerstein II sought to capture the dialect of its specific time and place—the Maine coastline, late nineteenth century. The language, therefore, was meticulously crafted, and used as a guide to the original company of actors, who were well trained in elocution.

Cast

Carrie Pipperidge .... Jean Darling
Julie Jordan .... Jan Clayton
Mrs. Mullin.. Jean Casto
Billy Bigelow ....John Raitt
Bessie ....Mimi Strongin
Jessie .... Jimsie Somers
Juggler... Lew Foldes
1st Policeman ....Robert Byrn
David Bascombe .... Franklyn Fox
Nettie Fowler ....Christine Johnson
June Girl ....Pearl Lang
Enoch Snow..................................... Eric Mattson
Jigger Craigin ....Murvyn Vye
Hannah.. Annabelle Lyon
Boatswain...Peter Birch
Arminy.. Connie Baxter
Penny ....Marilyn Merkt
Jennie .... Joan Keenan
Virginia ....Ginna Moise
Susan..Suzanne Tafel
Jonathan.. Richard H. Gordon
2nd Policeman .... Larry Evers
Captain .... Blake Ritter
1st Heavenly Friend
    (Brother Joshua)....................................Jay Velie
2nd Heavenly Friend........................... Tom Mcduffie
Starkeeper .... Russell Collins

Louise .... Bambi Linn
Carnival Boy ....Robert Pagent
Enoch Snow, Jr. .... Ralph Linn
Principal.. Lester Freedman

Singers: Martha Carver, Iva Withers, Anne Calvert, Connie Baxter, Glory Wills, Josephine Collins, Marilyn Merkt, Joan Keenan, Ginna Moise, Beatrice Miller, Suzanne Tafel, Verlyn Webb, Joseoh Bell, Robert Byrn, Tom Duffey, Blake Ritter, Charles Leighton, Louis Freed, Neil Chirico, Lester Freedman, Richard H. Gordon, and John Harrold

Dancers: Pearl Lang, Andrea Downing, Matgaret Cuddy, Polly Welch, Diane Chadwicke, Ruth Miller, Lu Lanterbar, Margaretta DeValera, Lynn Joelson, Sonia Joroff, Elena Salamatova, Marjory Svetlik, Ernest Richman, Tom Avera, Larry Evers, Ralph Linn, Tony Matthews, and David Ahdar

Production directed by Rouben Mamoulian
Dances by Agnes De Mille
Settings by Jo Mielziner
Costumes by Miles White
Production supervised by Lawrence Langner and Theresa Helburn
Musical Director, Joseph Littau
Ballet Arrangements by Trude Rittmann
Orchestrations by Don Walker

Synopsis of Scenes
TIME: 1873–1888

PRELUDE

An Amusement Park on the New England Coast. May. Waltz Prelude: "THE CAROUSEL WALTZ"

ACT 1

ACT 2

ACT 1

Scene 1

Waltz Prelude: "THE CAROUSEL WALTZ."

SCENE: *An Amusement Park on the New England Coast.*

TIME: *Late afternoon.*

Extending from stage right to the center is a merry-go-round labeled "Mullin's Carousel." Below the merry-go-round, right center, is the stand of Billy Bigelow, the barker for the carousel. Left center is the ticket-seller's stand where Mrs. Mullin herself presides. Up on the extreme left is a platform backed by an ornate show tent occupied by "The Beauties of Europe." Below this platform, down left, is another stand occupied by the barker for the "Beauties." The two barker stands are elevated so that these two characters can be easily seen above the heads of the crowd. MRS. MULLIN is seated on a high stool behind her stand so that she is also visible at all times. Downstage extreme right is a Hoky Poky Ice Cream wagon; a MAN standing upstage from it is selling ice-cream cornucopias.

NOTE: *This scene is set to the music of a waltz suite. The only sound comes from the orchestra pit. The pantomimic action is synchronized to the music, but it is in no sense a ballet treatment.*

AT RISE: FISHERMEN, SAILORS, THEIR WIVES, CHILDREN, GIRLS *from the local mill, and other types of a coastal town are seen moving about the park, patronizing the various concessions and in general "seeing the sights." The carousel is in full motion as the curtain rises, the "Three Beauties of Europe" are dancing on the platform, a juggler is busy juggling downstage left.* BILLY *is standing downstage of his stand and leaning against the stand just watching the proceedings. The whole stage seems to be alive and everyone is having a good time.*

Almost immediately we see the JUGGLER *cross to the center of the stage to juggle a hat on one stick and a plate on another. As he does this, the carousel comes to a stop. The* RIDERS *descend from their animals and leave the platform in all directions to mill around with the crowd. The "Three Beauties of Europe" stop dancing. They slip into robes for their rest period. One* KID *on the carousel during all this movement has stubbornly clung to his horse and neither his* MOTHER *nor his big* SISTER *can get him off. The* SISTER, *a tattletale type, skips happily across to her father, who is talking to another gentleman. She pulls at his sleeve and points to her rebellious brother* DAVID. MR. BASCOMBE, *a formidable fellow with sideburns on his cheeks and a heavy gold watch-chain across his belly, starts out with his daughter to aid his wife against his recalcitrant son. When he gets there he stands in back of* DAVID, JR., *with that stern look he reserves for such occasions. That's all there is to it.* DAVID *knows the jig is up. He gets off the horse, and the family now walk across the stage with the pomp that befits the richest clan in the locality. They own the Bascombe Cotton Mills, "a little ways up the river." Several people greet them with respectful awe, and they return a gracious but dignified bow to all.*

The JUGGLER, *center stage, has by this time stopped juggling and one of the dancers on the platform has come down and is passing a hat among the crowd for a little collection. As the* JUGGLER *goes back to his corner down left, we see a* GIRL *and a* SAILOR *enter from right. They cross down in front of* BILLY. *She decides she wants to talk to him, so she crosses to her sailor friend and asks him to buy her some ice cream. The* SAILOR *crosses to the ice-cream wagon to buy the cones, and as he does, the* GIRL *crosses to* BILLY *and talks to him. The* SAILOR, *having bought the cones, crosses back to the spot where he was, but sees no girl. He turns upstage, sees her flirting with* BILLY. *Crossing up between the two, he looks angrily at* BILLY, *turns to his girl, and tells her to hold the cones. She does. The sailor turns to* BILLY *and is just about to take a good sock at him when he notices that* BILLY *towers over him.* BILLY *smiles and the sailor's look is now one of "I'd better leave this guy alone." He saunters off to the left with his girl.* BILLY *then crosses up to* MRS. MULLIN, *a small group of adoring young females following his every movement with worshipful eyes.* MRS. MULLIN *is completely mollified by the little attention and gives him a nice big hug.*

CARRIE *and* JULIE *enter from down left.* CARRIE *is a naïve, direct, and normal young woman of the period.* JULIE *is more complex, quieter, deeper. They look around at the gay sights, two mill girls on an afternoon off.* JULIE *crosses to right center.* CARRIE *is mixing in with the crowd left center when* BILLY *crosses to go back to his stand down right. On the way he nearly bumps into Julie. Their eyes meet for a moment. Then he goes on.*

About this time the BARKER *of "The Beauties of Europe" comes out and gets on this stand and tries to attract the crowd by pointing to his weary dancers. But now* BILLY *starts his spiel and the entire stageful turns toward him and the carousel while* MRS. MULLIN, *the proprietress, beams above them. Everyone on the stage starts to sway unconsciously with the rhythm of* BILLY's *words (unheard by the audience)—all but* JULIE. JULIE *just stands, looking at him over the heads of the others, her gaze steady, her body motionless.* BILLY *becomes conscious of her. He looks curiously at her. She takes his mind off his work. He mechanically repeats his spiel. The heads turned up at him now follow his eyes and turn slowly toward* JULIE. *This is also the direction of "The Beauties of Europe," and the enterprising* BARKER *of that attraction immediately takes advantage of this and starts his dancers dancing feverishly, doing bumps that they probably learned at Coney Island. The crowd is now completely "Beauty"-conscious.* BILLY *is* JULIE-*conscious and gets down off his stand.* MRS. MULLIN, *realizing the situation, runs over to* BILLY *and seems to shout up at him.*

BILLY *comes to. His barker's pride reawakened, he mounts his stand and proceeds to win back his public. He starts his regular spiel. The girls all turn back to* BILLY *and sway with his rhythm again. Some of the men go along with the "Beauties"—all except the ones whose wives pull them away.*

When BILLY *finishes, there is a stampede of girls to buy tickets for the carousel.* JULIE *tries too, but she gets crowded out.* BILLY *notices this; pretty soon there will be no more places left. He smiles and with exaggerated gallantry walks over to her and offers his arm. With a frightened little grin she accepts it and he leads her grandly toward the carousel.* MRS. MULLIN, *her nose out of joint, yells at* JULIE, *motioning to her that she wants her five-cent fare.*

JULIE *fumbles in her purse. After some delay, occasioned by her excitement, she finally produces a nickel. Then* MRS. MULLIN *takes her time about giving her a ticket. In fact, she stalls until the carousel actually gets started. When she has her ticket, Julie dashes back to the carousel. It is going slowly and she is afraid to get on.* BILLY *laughs and suddenly lifts her up and puts her on the only remaining horse on the carousel.*

(It must be understood that BILLY's *attitude to* JULIE *throughout this scene is one of only casual and laconic interest. He can get all the girls he wants. One is like another. This one is a cute little thing. Like hundreds of others)*

Once he has got her on the carousel, he dismisses her from his mind. He turns back to MRS. MULLIN, *but for some reason that lady gives him an icy glare. He shrugs his shoulders, looks again to the carousel, and collects the tickets from the people seated on the various animals.* JULIE *comes around again. He waves at her patronizingly. It means nothing to him. She waves back. It means so much to her that she nearly falls off! He laughs. The carousel is revolving faster now, but he hops on and leans against the horse on which* JULIE *is* seated. MRS. MULLIN, *seeing this, is so furious that she gets down from her stand and starts to pace the stage angrily. Great excitement is stirring down right. A group of* KIDS *herald the approach of a bear being led on stage by a* BALLERINA *in a short ruffly skirt. (The bear is a small man in a well-made bearskin.)*

Arriving stage center, the girl in the ruffly skirt executes a few dance steps. Then, to the great delight of all, the BEAR *does exactly the same steps. A* CLOWN *now enters from down right, goes on stage next to the* BEAR, *and does some acrobatic tricks. The* JUGGLER *starts juggling again, the dancers dance. The entire stage is in a bedlam of excitement, the carousel keeps turning at full speed,* BILLY *is leaning closer to* JULIE, *the music rises in an ecstatic crescendo, but the lights, as if they sensed that we have accomplished all we wanted to in this scene, black out and the curtains close.*

Scene 2

SCENE: *A tree-lined path along the shore. A few minutes later. Near sundown. Through the trees the lights of the amusement park can be seen on the curves of the bay.*
The music of the merry-go-round is heard faintly in the distance.

AT RISE: *There is a park bench just right of center. Soon after the curtain rises,* CARRIE *backs on to the stage from down right, followed by* JULIE.

CARRIE

C'mon, Julie, it's gettin' late . . . Julie! That's right! Don't you pay her no mind.
        (*Looking off stage*)
Look! She's comin' at you again. Let's run!

JULIE
        (*Holding her ground*)

I ain't skeered o' her.
        (*But she is a little.*)

MRS. MULLIN
        (*Entering, in no mood to be trifled with*)

I got one more thing to tell you, young woman. If y'ever so much as poke your nose in my carousel again, you'll be thrown out. Right on your little pink behind!

CARRIE

You got no call t'talk t'her like that! She ain't doin' you no harm.

MRS. MULLIN

Oh, ain't she? Think I wanta get in trouble with the police and lose my license?

JULIE
(*To* CARRIE)

What is the woman talkin' about?

MRS. MULLIN
(*Scornfully*)

Lettin' my barker fool with you! Ain't you ashamed?

JULIE

I don't let no man . . .

MRS. MULLIN
(*To* CARRIE)

He leaned against her all through the ride.

JULIE
(*To* CARRIE)

He leaned against the horse. (*To* MRS. MULLIN) But he didn't lay a hand on me!

MRS. MULLIN

Oh, no, Miss Innercence! And he didn't put his arm around yer waist neither.

CARRIE

And suppose he did. Is that a reason to hev a capuluptic fit?

MRS. MULLIN

You keep out o' this, you rip! (*To* JULIE) You've had my warnin'.
If you come back you'll be thrown out!

JULIE

Who'll throw me out?

MRS. MULLIN

Billy Bigelow—the barker. Same feller you let get so free with
you.

JULIE

I—I bet he wouldn't. He wouldn't throw me out!

CARRIE

I bet the same thing.
    (BILLY BIGELOW *enters, followed by* TWO GIRLS. *He hears
and sees the argument; he turns and tells the girls to leave.
They exit.*)

MRS. MULLIN
(*To* CARRIE)

You mind your business, hussy!

CARRIE

Go back to yer carousel and leave us alone!

JULIE

Yes. Leave us alone, y'old—y'old—

MRS. MULLIN

I don't run my business for a lot o' chippies.

CARRIE

Chippy, yerself!

JULIE

Yes, Chippy yerself!

BILLY
(*Shouting*)

Shut up! Jabber jabber jabber! . . . (*They stand before him like three guilty schoolgirls. He makes his voice shrill to imitate them*) Jabber jabber jabber jabber jabber . . . What's goin' on anyway? Spittin' and sputt'rin'—like three lumps of corn poppin' on a shovel!

JULIE

Mr. Bigelow, please—

BILLY

Don't yell!

JULIE
(*Backing away a step*)

I didn't yell.

BILLY

Well—don't. (*To* MRS. MULLIN) What's the matter?

MRS. MULLIN

Take a look at that girl, Billy. She ain't ever to be allowed on my carousel again. Next time she tries to get in—if she ever dares— I want you to throw her out! Understand? Throw her out!

BILLY
(*Turning to* JULIE)
All right. You heard what the lady said. Run home now.

CARRIE
C'mon, Julie.

JULIE
(*Looking at* BILLY, *amazed*)
No, I won't.

MRS. MULLIN
(*To* BILLY)
Like a drink?

BILLY
Sure.

JULIE
(*Speaking very earnestly, as if it meant a great deal to her*)
Mr. Bigelow, tell me please—honest and truly—if I came to the
carousel, would you throw me out?
(*He looks at* MRS. MULLIN, *then at* JULIE, *then back at* MRS.
MULLIN)

BILLY
What did she do, anyway?

JULIE
She says you put your arm around my waist.

BILLY
(*The light dawning on him*)

So that's it! (*Turning to* MRS. MULLIN) Here's something new! Can't put my arm around a girl without I ask your permission! That how it is?

MRS. MULLIN
(*For the first time on the defensive*)
I just don't want that one around no more.

BILLY
(*Turning to* JULIE)
You come round all you want, see? And if y'ain't got the price Billy Bigelow'll treat you to a ride.

MRS. MULLIN
Big talker, ain't you, Mr. Bigelow? I suppose you think I can't throw *you* out too, if I wanta! (BILLY, *ignoring her, looks straight ahead of him, complacently*) You're such a good barker I can't get along without you. That it? Well, just for that you're discharged. Your services are no longer required. You're bounced! See?

BILLY
Very well, Mrs. Mullin.

MRS. MULLIN
(*In retreat*)
You know I *could* bounce you if I felt like it!

BILLY
And you felt like it just now. So I'm bounced.

MRS. MULLIN
Do you have to pick up every word I say? I only said—

BILLY

That my services were no longer required. Very good. We'll let it go at that, Mrs. Mullin.

MRS. MULLIN

All right, you devil! (*Shouting*) We'll let it go at that!

JULIE

Mr. Bigelow, if she's willin' to say she'll change her mind—

BILLY

You keep out of it.

JULIE

I don't want this to happen 'count of me.

BILLY
(*Suddenly, to* MRS. MULLIN, *pointing at* JULIE)
Apologize to her!

CARRIE

A—ha!

MRS. MULLIN

Me apologize to *her*! Fer what? Fer spoilin' the good name of my carousel—the business that was left to me by my dear, saintly, departed husband, Mr. Mullin? (*Led toward tears by her own eloquence*) I only wish my poor husband was alive this minute.

BILLY

I bet *he* don't.

MRS. MULLIN

He'd give you such a smack on the jaw—!

BILLY

That's just what *I'm* goin' to give you if you don't dry up!
(*He advances threateningly*)

MRS. MULLIN
(*Backing away*)

You upstart! After all I done for you! Now I'm through with you
for good! Y'hear?

BILLY
(*Making as if to take a swipe at her with the back of his hand*)

Get!

MRS. MULLIN
(*As she goes off*)

Through fer good! I won't take you back like before!
(BILLY *watches her go, then crosses back to* JULIE. *There is a
moment of awkward silence*)

CARRIE

Mr. Bigelow—

BILLY

Don't get sorry for me or I'll give *you* a slap on the jaw! (*More
silence. He looks at* JULIE. *She lowers her eyes*) And don't *you* feel
sorry for me either!

JULIE
(*Frightened*)

I don't feel sorry for you, Mr. Bigelow.

BILLY

You're a liar, you *are* feelin' sorry for me. I can see it in your face. (*Faces front, throws out chest, proud*) You think, now that she fired me, I won't be able to get another job . . .

JULIE

What *will* you do now, Mr. Bigelow?

BILLY

First of all, I'll go get myself—a glass of beer. Whenever anything bothers me I always drink a glass of beer.

JULIE

Then you are bothered about losing your job!

BILLY

No. Only about how I'm goin' t'pay fer the beer. (*To* CARRIE, *gesturing with right hand*) Will you pay for it? (CARRIE *looks doubtful, he speaks to* JULIE) Will you? (JULIE *doesn't answer*) How much money have you got?

JULIE

Forty-three cents.

BILLY

(*To* CARRIE)

And you? (CARRIE *lowers her eyes and turns left*) I asked you how much you've got? (CARRIE *begins to weep softly*) Uh, I understand. Well, you needn't cry about it . . . I'm goin' to the carousel to get my things. Stay here till I come back. Then we'll go have a drink. (JULIE *is fumbling for change. She holds it up to* BILLY) It's all right. (*He pushes her hand gently away*) Keep your money, I'll pay.

(*He exits whistling down right.* JULIE *continues to look silently off at the departing figure of* BILLY. CARRIE *studies her for a moment, then timidly opens the subject of her interest by calling* JULIE's *name. She crosses to bench left of* JULIE *and sits.*)

CARRIE

Julie—(*No answer. From here the lines are synchronized to music*)
Julie—Do you like him?

JULIE
(*Dreaming*)

I dunno.
(*She sits on bench.*)

CARRIE

Did you like it when he talked to you today?
When he put you on the carousel, that way?
Did you like that?

JULIE

'D ruther not say.

CARRIE
(*Shakes her head and chides her*)

You're a queer one, Julie Jordan!
You are quieter and deeper than a well,
And you never tell me nothin'—

JULIE

There's nothin' that I keer t'choose t'tell!

CARRIE

You been actin' most peculiar!

Ev'ry mornin' you're awake ahead of me,
Alw'ys settin' by the winder—

JULIE

I like to watch the river meet the sea.

CARRIE

When we work in the mill, weavin' at the loom,
Y'gaze absent-minded at the roof,
And half the time yer shuttle gets twisted in the threads
Till y'can't tell the warp from the woof!

JULIE
(*Looking away and smiling. She knows it's true*)
'T ain't so!

CARRIE

You're a queer one, Julie Jordan!
You won't ever tell a body what you think.
You're as tight-lipped as an oyster,
And as silent as an old Sahaira Spink!

JULIE

Spinx.
(*These lines are spoken over music*)

CARRIE

Huh?

JULIE

Spinx.

CARRIE

Uh-uh. Spink.

JULIE

Y'spell it with an "x."

CARRIE

That's only when there's more than one.

JULIE
(*Outbluffed*)

Oh.

CARRIE
(*Looking sly*)

Julie, I been bustin' t'tell *you* somethin' lately.

JULIE

Y'hev?

CARRIE

Reason I didn't keer t'tell you before was 'cause you din't hev a feller of yer own. Now y'got one, I ken tell y'about mine.

JULIE
(*Quietly, and thoughtfully*)

I'm glad you got a feller, Carrie. What's his name?

CARRIE
(*Now she sings, almost reverently*)

His name is Mister Snow,
And an upstandin' man is he.

He comes home ev'ry night in his round-bottomed boat
With a net full of herring from the sea.

An almost perfect beau,
As refined as a girl could wish,
But he spends so much time in his round-bottomed boat
That he can't seem to lose the smell of fish!

The fust time he kissed me, the whiff of his clo'es
Knocked me flat on the floor of the room;
But now that I love him, my heart's in my nose,
And fish is my fav'rit perfume!
Last night he spoke quite low,
And a fair-spoken man is he,
    (*Memorizing exactly what he said*)
And he said, "Miss Pipperidge, I'd like it fine
If I could be wed with a wife.
And, indeed, Miss Pipperidge, if you'll be mine,
I'll be yours fer the rest of my life."

Next moment we were promised!
And now my mind's in a maze,
Fer all I ken do is look forward to
That wonderful day of days . . .

When I marry Mister Snow,
The flowers'll be buzzin' with the hum of bees,
The birds'll make a racket in the churchyard trees,
When I marry Mister Snow.

Then it's off to home we'll go,
And both of us'll look a little dreamy-eyed,
A-drivin' to a cottage by the oceanside

Where the salty breezes blow.
He'll carry me 'cross the threshold,
And I'll be meek as a lamb.
Then he'll set me on my feet
And I'll say, kinda sweet:
"Well, Mister Snow, here I am!"

Then I'll kiss him so he'll know
That ev'rythin'll be as right as right ken be
A-livin' in a cottage by the sea with me,
For I love that Mister Snow—
That young, seafarin', bold and darin',
Big, bewhiskered, overbearin' darlin', *Mister Snow!*
   (*She looks soulfully ahead of her, and sits down, in a trance of her own making.*)

JULIE

Carrie! I'm so happy fer you!

CARRIE

So y'see I ken understand now how *you* feel about Billy Bigelow.
   (BILLY *enters down right, carrying a suitcase and with a coat on his arm. He puts the suitcase down and the coat on top of it.*)

BILLY

You still here?
   (*They both rise, looking at* BILLY.)

CARRIE

You *told* us to wait fer you.

BILLY

What you think I want with two of you? I meant that *one* of you
was to wait. The other can go home.

CARRIE

All right.

JULIE
(*Almost simultaneously*)

All right.
(*They look at each other, then at* BILLY, *smiling inanely.*)

BILLY

One of you goes home.
(*To* CARRIE)
Where do you work?

CARRIE

Bascombe's Cotton Mill, a little ways up the river.

BILLY

And you?

JULIE

I work there, too.

BILLY

Well, one of you goes home. Which of you wants to stay?
(*No answer.*)
Come on, speak up! Which of you stays?

CARRIE

Whoever stays loses her job.

BILLY

How do you mean?

CARRIE

All Bascombe's girls hev to be respectable. We all hev to live in the mill boarding-house, and if we're late they lock us out and we can't go back to work there any more.

BILLY

Is that true? Will they bounce you if you're not home on time? (*Both girls nod.*)

JULIE

That's right.

CARRIE

Julie, should I go?

JULIE

I—can't tell you what to do.

CARRIE

All right—you stay, if y'like.

BILLY

That right, you'll be discharged if you stay? (JULIE *nods.*)

CARRIE

Julie, should I go?

JULIE
(*Embarrassed*)
Why do you keep askin' me that?

CARRIE
You know what's best to do.

JULIE
(*Profoundly moved, slowly*)
All right, Carrie, you can go home.
(*Pause. Then reluctantly,* CARRIE *starts off. As she gets left center,
she turns and says, uncertainly:*)

CARRIE
Well, good night.
(*She waits a moment to see if* JULIE *will follow her.* JULIE *doesn't
move.* CARRIE *exits.*)

BILLY
(*Speaking as he crosses to left center*)
Now we're both out of a job. (*No answer. He whistles softly.*)
Have you had your supper?

JULIE
No.

BILLY
Want to eat out on the pier?

JULIE
No.

BILLY

Anywhere's else?

JULIE

No.

(*He whistles a few more bars. He sits on the bench, looking her over, up and down.*)

BILLY

You don't come to the carousel much. Only see you three times before today.

JULIE

(*She crosses to bench and sits beside him*)

I been there much more than that.

BILLY

That right? Did you see me?

JULIE

Yes.

BILLY

Did you know I was Billy Bigelow?

JULIE

They told me.

(*He whistles again, then turns to her.*)

BILLY

Have you got a sweetheart?

JULIE

No.

BILLY

Ah, don't lie to me.

JULIE

I haven't anybody.

BILLY

You stayed here with me first time I asked you. You know your way around all right, all right!

JULIE

No, I don't, Mr. Bigelow.

BILLY

And I suppose you don't know why you're sittin' here—like this—alone with me. You wouldn' of stayed so quick if you hadna done it before . . . What did you stay for, anyway?

JULIE

So you wouldn't be left alone.

BILLY

Alone! God, you're dumb! I don't need to be alone. I can have all the girls I want. Don't you know that?

JULIE

I know, Mr. Bigelow.

BILLY

What do you know?

JULIE

That all the girls are crazy fer you. But that's not why *I* stayed. I stayed because you been so good to me.

BILLY

Well, then you can go home.

JULIE

I don't want to go home now.

BILLY

And suppose I go away and leave you sittin' here?

JULIE

Even then I wouldn't go home.

BILLY

Do you know what you remind me of? A girl I knew in Coney Island. Tell you how I met her. One night at closin' time—we had put out the lights in the carousel, and just as I was—
> (*He breaks off suddenly as, during the above speech, a* POLICE-MAN *has entered and comes across stage.* BILLY *instinctively takes on an attitude of guilty silence. The* POLICEMAN *frowns down at them as he walks by.* BILLY *follows him with his eyes. At the same time that the* POLICEMAN *entered,* MR. BASCOMBE *has come in. He flourishes his cane and breathes in the night air as if he enjoyed it.*)

POLICEMAN

Evenin', Mr. Bascombe.

BASCOMBE

Good evening, Timony. Nice night.

POLICEMAN

'Deed it is. (*Whispers into* BASCOMBE's *ear*) Er—Mr. Bascombe.
That girl is one of your girls.

BASCOMBE

(*In a low voice*)

One of my girls? (*The* POLICEMAN *nods.* BASCOMBE *crosses in front of the* POLICEMAN *to* JULIE *and peers at her in the darkness*) Is that you, Miss Jordan?

JULIE

Yes, Mr. Bascombe.

BASCOMBE

What ever are you doing out at this hour?

JULIE

I—I—

BASCOMBE

You know what time we close our doors at the mill boarding-house. You couldn't be home on time now if you ran all the way.

JULIE

No, sir.

BILLY

(*To* JULIE)

Who's old sideburns?

POLICEMAN

Here, now! Don't you go t'callin' Mr. Bascombe names—'Less you're fixin' t'git yerself into trouble. (BILLY *shuts up. Policemen have this effect on him. The* POLICEMAN *turns to* BASCOMBE.) We got a report on this feller from the police chief at Bangor. He's a pretty fly gazaybo. Come up from Coney Island.

BASCOMBE

New York, eh?

POLICEMAN

He works on carousels, makes a specialty of young things like this'n. Gets 'em all mooney-eyed. Promises to marry 'em, then takes their money.

JULIE
(*Promptly and brightly*)

I ain't got any money.

POLICEMAN

Speak when you're spoken to, miss!

BASCOMBE

Julie, you've heard what kind of blackguard this man is. You're an inexperienced girl and he's imposed on you and deluded you. That's why I'm inclined to give you one more chance.

POLICEMAN
(*To* JULIE)

Y'hear that?

BASCOMBE

I'm meeting Mrs. Bascombe at the church. We'll drive you home and I'll explain everything to the house matron. (*He holds out his hand*) Come, my child. (*But she doesn't move*)

POLICEMAN

Well, girl! Don't be settin' there like you didn't hev good sense!

JULIE

Do I *hev* to go with you?

BASCOMBE

No. You don't have to.

JULIE

Then I'll stay.

POLICEMAN

After I warned you!

BASCOMBE

You see, Timony! There are some of them you just can't help. Good night!
(*He exits.*)

POLICEMAN

Good night, Mr. Bascombe. (*He looks down at* BILLY, *starts to go, then turns to* BILLY *and speaks*) You! You low-down scalawag! I oughta throw you in jail.

BILLY

What for?

POLICEMAN
(*After a pause*)

Dunno. Wish I did.
(*He exits.* BILLY *looks after him.*)

JULIE

Well, and *then* what?

BILLY

Huh?

JULIE

You were startin' to tell me a story.

BILLY

Me?

JULIE

About that girl in Coney Island. You said you just put out the lights in the carousel—that's as far as you got.

BILLY

Oh, yes. Yes, well, just as the lights went out, someone came along. A little girl with a shawl—you know, she—(*Puzzled*) Say, tell me somethin'—ain't you scared of me? (*Music starts here*)
    I mean, after what the cop said about me takin' money from girls.

JULIE

I ain't skeered.

BILLY

That your name? Julie? Julie somethin'?

JULIE

Julie Jordan.
        (BILLY *whistles reflectively.*)

BILLY
(*Singing softly, shaking head*)
You're a queer one, Julie Jordan.
Ain't you sorry that you didn't run away?
You can still go, if you wanta—

JULIE
(*Singing, looking away so as not to meet his eye*)
I reckon that I keer t'choose t'stay.
You couldn't take my money
If I didn't *hev* any,
And I don't hev a penny, that's true!
And if I did *hev* money
You couldn't take any
'Cause you'd ask, and I'd give it to you!

BILLY
(*Singing*)
You're a queer one, Julie Jordan . . .
Ain't y'ever had a feller you give money to?

JULIE
No.

BILLY
Ain't y'ever had a feller at all?

JULIE
No.

BILLY
Well y'musta had a feller you went walkin' with—

JULIE

Yes.

BILLY

Where'd you walk?

JULIE

Nowhere special I recall.

BILLY

In the woods?

JULIE

No.

BILLY

On the beach?

JULIE

No.

BILLY

Did you love him?

JULIE

No! Never loved no one—I *told* you that!

BILLY

Say, you're a funny kid. Want to go into town and dance maybe?
Or—

JULIE

No. I have to be keerful.

BILLY

Of what?

JULIE

My character. Y'see, I'm never goin' to marry.
    (*Singing*)
    I'm never goin' to marry.
    If I was goin' to marry,
    I wouldn't hev t'be sech a stickler.
    But I'm never goin' to marry,
    And a girl who don't marry
    Hes got to be much more pertickler!
    (*Following lines spoken*)

BILLY

Suppose I was to say to you that I'd marry you?

JULIE

You?

BILLY

That scares you, don't it? You're thinkin' what that cop said.

JULIE

No, I ain't. I never paid no mind to what he said.

BILLY

But you wouldn't marry anyone like me, would you?

JULIE

Yes, I would, if I loved you. It wouldn't make any difference what you—even if I died fer it.

BILLY

How do you know what you'd do if you loved me? Or how you'd feel—or anythin'?

JULIE

I dunno how I know.

BILLY

Ah—

JULIE

Jest the same, I know how I—how it'd be—if I loved you.
  (*Singing*)
    When I worked in the mill, weavin' at the loom,
    I'd gaze absent-minded at the roof,
    And half the time the shuttle'd tangle in the threads,
    And the warp'd get mixed with the woof . . .
    If I loved you—

BILLY
(*Spoken*)

But you don't.

JULIE
(*Spoken*)

No I don't . . .
  (*Smiles and sings*)
    But somehow I ken see
    Jest exackly how I'd be . . .

    If I loved you,
    Time and again I would try to say

All I'd want you to know.
If I loved you,
Words wouldn't come in an easy way—
Round in circles I'd go!
Longin' to tell you, but afraid and shy,
I'd let my golden chances pass me by.
Soon you'd leave me,
Off you would go in the mist of day,
Never, never to know
How I loved you—
If I loved you.
    (*Pause*)

BILLY

Well, anyway—you don't love me. That's what you said.

JULIE

Yes . . . I can smell them, can you? The blossoms. (BILLY *picks some blossoms up and drops them*) The wind brings them down.

BILLY

Ain't *much* wind tonight. Hardly any.
    (*Singing*)
    You can't hear a sound—not the turn of a leaf,
    Nor the fall of a wave, hittin' the sand.
    The tide's creepin' up on the beach like a thief,
    Afraid to be caught stealin' the land.
    On a night like this I start to wonder what life is all about.

JULIE

And I always say two heads are better than one, to figger it out.

BILLY
(*Spoken over short musical interlude*)
I don't need you or anyone to help me. I got it figgered out for myself. We ain't important. What are we? A couple of specks of nothin'. Look up there.
(*He points up. They both look up.*)
(*He sings*)
There's a helluva lot o' stars in the sky,
And the sky's so big the sea looks small,
And two little people—
You and I—
We don't count at all.
(*They are silent for a while, the music continuing.* BILLY *looks down at her and speaks.*)
You're a funny kid. Don't remember ever meetin' a girl like you. (*A thought strikes him suddenly. He looks suspicious. He lets her hand go and backs away.*) You—are you tryin' t'get me to marry you?

JULIE
No.

BILLY
Then what's puttin' it into my head? (*He thinks it out. She smiles. He looks down at her*) You're different all right. Don't know what it is. (*Holds her chin in his right hand*) You look up at me with that little kid face like—like you trusted me. (*She looks at him steadily, smiling sadly, as if she were sorry for him and wanted to help him. He looks thoughtful, then talks to himself, but audibly.*) I wonder what it'd be like.

JULIE
What?

BILLY

Nothin'. (*To himself again*) I know what it'd be like. It'd be awful. I can just see myself—
(*He sings*)
Kinda scawny and pale, pickin' at my food,
And lovesick like any other guy—
I'd throw away my sweater and dress up like a dude
In a dickey and a collar and a tie . . .
If I loved you—

JULIE
(*Speaking*)

But you don't.

BILLY
(*Speaking*)

No I don't.
(*Singing*)
But somehow I can see
Just exactly how I'd be.

If I loved you,
Time and again I would try to say
All I'd want you to know.
If I loved you,
Words wouldn't come in an easy way—
Round in circles I'd go!
Longing to tell you, but afraid and shy,
I'd let my golden chances pass me by.
Soon you'd leave me,
Off you would go in the mist of day,
Never, never to know
How I loved you—

If I loved you.
(*He thinks it over for a few silent moments. Then he shakes his head ruefully. He turns to* JULIE *and frowns at her. The rest of the scene is spoken over music*)
I'm not a feller to marry anybody. Even if a girl was foolish enough to want me to, I wouldn't.

JULIE
(*Looking right up at him*)
Don't worry about it—Billy.

BILLY
Who's worried!
(*She smiles and looks up at the trees.*)

JULIE
You're right about there bein' no wind. The blossom are jest comin' down by theirselves. Jest their time to, I reckon.
(BILLY *looks straight ahead of him, a troubled expression in his eyes.* JULIE *looks up at him, smiling, patient. The music rises ecstatically. He crosses nearer to her and looks down at her. She doesn't move her eyes from his. He takes her face in his hands, leans down, and kisses her gently. The curtains close as the lights dim.*)

Scene 3

SCENE: *Nettie Fowler's Spa on the ocean front. June. Up right is Nettie's establishment (and residence combined) of gray, weathered clapboard and shingled roof. Just left of the door, on the porch, there is a good-sized arbor, overhung with wisteria. Under the arbor are a table and three chairs. From the house to off-stage left platforms are built up and appear to be docks. The backdrop, painted blue, depicts the bay. On the drop is painted a moored ketch and other sailing craft.*

AT RISE: *Men carrying bushel baskets of clams and piling them on the dock, preparatory to loading the boats. During the scene more men come on.*

A group stand outside the spa to heckle NETTIE *and the women who are inside, cooking. Other men enter and join the hecklers.*

Music continues, but the first lines are not sung or metrically synchronized.

1ST MAN

Nettie!

2ND MAN
(Cupping his hands and calling off)

Oh, Nettie Fowler!

NETTIE
(In the house)

Hold yer horses!

1ST MAN

Got any of them doughnuts fried yet?

3RD MAN

How 'bout some apple turnovers.

NETTIE
(*Still inside, getting irritated*)

Hold yer horses!
(*The men laugh, now that they're getting a rise out of her*)

2ND MAN
(*Crossing up to porch*)

Hey, what're you and them women doin' in there?

WOMEN
(*Off*)

Hold yer horses!
(*The men slap their thighs, and one another's backs. This is rich!*)

1ST MAN

Are y'cookin' the ice cream?
(*This convulses them. Throws his arm on 3rd man's shoulders*)

3RD MAN

Roastin' the lemonade?

ALL MEN

Nettie Fowler!
Yoo-hoo!
Nettie Fow-w-w-w-ler!
(*Some* WOMEN *come out of the house.* CARRIE *follows, pushing her way through the crowd and coming up front. The* GIRLS *carry rolling-pins and spoons—a formidable crowd of angry females interrupted at their work in the kitchen. Their stern looks soon reduce the male laughter to faint snickers and sheepish grins.*)

SEVERAL GIRLS

Will you stop that racket!

CARRIE

Git away, you passel o'demons!

1ST MAN

Where's Nettie?

CARRIE

In the kitchen busier'n a bee in a bucket o'tar—and y'oughter be ashamed, makin' yersel's a plague and a nuisance with yer yellin' and screamin' and carryin' on.
(From here on, the dialogue is sung, unless otherwise indicated.)

GIRLS

Give it to 'em good, Carrie,
Give it to 'em good!

CARRIE

Get away, you no-account nothin's
With yer silly jokes and prattle!
If y'packed all yer brains in a butterfly's head
They'd still hev room to rattle.

GIRLS

Give it to 'em good, Carrie,
Give it to 'em good!
Tell 'em somethin' that'll l'arn 'em!

CARRIE

Get away, you roustabout riff-raff,
With yer bellies full of grog.

If y'packed all yer brains in a polywog's head,
He'd never even grow to be a frog!

GIRLS

The polywog'd never be a frog!
That'll l'arn 'em, darn 'em!

ALL MEN

Now jest a minute, ladies,
You got no call to fret.
We only asked perlitely
If you was ready yet.

We'd kinda like this clambake
To get an early start,
And wanted fer to tell you
We went and done our part.

BASSES
(*Pointing to a pile of baskets*)

Look at them clams!

BARITONES

Been diggin' 'em since sunup!

BASSES

Look at them clams!

TENORS

All ready fer the boats.

ALL MEN

Diggin' them clams,

TENORS

We're all wore out and done up—

ALL

And what's more we're as hungry as goats!

ALL GIRLS

You'll get no drinks er vittles
Till we get across the bay,
So pull in yer belts
And load them boats
And let's get under way.

The sooner we sail,
The sooner we start
The clambake across the bay!

(*They snap their fingers and turn. But the boys' attention has been caught by the entrance of* NETTIE, *coming out of the house carrying a tray piled high with doughnuts. She is followed by a* LITTLE GIRL, *carrying a large tray of coffee cups.*)

(*The following lines are spoken.*)

NETTIE

Here, boys: Here's some doughnuts and coffee. Fall to!
(*Crosses to center.*)

MEN
(*As they fall to, speeches overlapping*)

Doughnuts, hooray!
That's our Nettie!
Yer heart's in the right place, Nettie!

Lemme in there!

Quit yer shovin'!

NETTIE

Here now, don't jump at it like you was a lotta animals in a menag'ry!

(*She laughs as she crosses over to the* GIRLS.)

GIRLS

Nettie! After us jest tellin' 'em! Whatcher doin' that fer?

NETTIE

They been diggin' clams since five this mornin'—I see 'em myself, down on the beach.

GIRLS

After the way they been pesterin' and annoyin' you!

CARRIE

Nettie, yer a soft-hearted ninny!

NETTIE

Oh, y'can't blame 'em. First clambake o' the year they're always like this. It's like unlockin' a door, and all the crazy notions they kep' shet up fer the winter come whoopin' out into the sunshine. This year's jest like ev'ry other.

(*The following line are sung*)

March went out like a lion,

A-whippin' up the water in the bay.

Then April cried

And stepped aside,

And along come pretty little May!

May was full of promises
But she didn't keep 'em quick enough fer some,
And a crowd of Doubtin' Thomases
Was predictin' that the summer'd never come!

MEN SINGERS

But it's comin', by gum!
Y'ken feel it come!
Y'ken feel it in yer heart,
Y'ken see it in the ground!
Y'ken hear it in the trees,
Y'ken smell it in the breeze—

ALL

Look around, look around, look around!

NETTIE

June is bustin' out all over,
All over the meadow and the hill!
Buds're bustin' outa bushes,
And the rompin' river pushes
Ev'ry little wheel that wheels beside a mill.

ALL

June is bustin' out all over.

NETTIE

The feelin' is gettin' so intense,
That the young Virginia creepers
Hev been huggin' the bejeepers
Outa all the mornin'-glories on the fence.
Because it's June!

MEN
June, June, June—

ALL
Jest because it's June—
June—Ju-u-une!

NETTIE
Fresh and alive and gay and young,
June is a love song, sweetly sung.

ALL
(*Softly*)
June is bustin' out all over!

MAN
The saplin's are bustin' out with sap!

GIRL
Love hes found my brother, Junior—

2ND MAN
And my sister's even lunier!

2ND GIRL
And my ma is gettin' kittenish with Pap!

ALL
June is bustin' out all over!

NETTIE
To ladies the men are payin' court.
Lotsa ships are kept at anchor

Jest because the captains hanker
Fer a comfort they ken only get in port!

ALL

Because it's June!
June—June—June—
Jest because it's June—June—Ju-u-ne!

NETTIE

June makes the bay look bright and new,
Sails gleaming white on sunlit blue—

CARRIE

June is bustin' out all over,
The ocean is full of Jacks and Jills.
With her little tail a-swishin'
Ev'ry lady fish is wishin'
That a male would come and grab her by the gills!

ALL

June is bustin' out all over!

NETTIE

The sheep aren't sleepin' any more.
All the rams that chase the ewe sheep
Are determined there'll be new sheep
And the ewe sheep aren't even keepin' score!

ALL

On accounta it's June!
June—June—June—
Jest because it's June—

June—
June!

NETTIE

June is bustin' out all over,
All over the beaches ev'ry night.
From Pennobscot to Augusty
All the boys are feelin' lusty,
And the girls ain't even puttin' up a fight.

ALL

Because it's June,
June, June, June,
Jest because it's June! June! June!
(*Dance. After the dance all exit except* NETTIE, CARRIE, *and a small group of* GIRLS. JULIE *enters.*)

CARRIE

Hello, Julie.

NETTIE

Did you find him?

JULIE

No. (*Explaining to* CARRIE) He went out with Jigger Craigin last night and he didn't come home.

CARRIE

Jigger Craigin?

JULIE

His new friend—he's a sailor on that big whaler, the *Nancy B.* She's sailing tomorrow. I'll be glad.

NETTIE

Why don't you two visit for a while. (*Necks are craned, ears cocked.* NETTIE *notices this.*) Look, girls, we got work to do. C'mon. You sweep those steps up there. (*Herding the* GIRLS *upstage*) You set up there and keep outa the way and don't poke yer noses in other people's business.

JULIE

You need me, Cousin Nettie?

NETTIE

No. You stay out here and visit with Carrie. You haven't seen each other fer a long time. Do you good.
        (*She exits into the house.* JULIE *and* CARRIE *sit on the bait box,* JULIE *right of* CARRIE. *All ears are open upstage.*)

CARRIE

Is he workin' yet?

JULIE

No. Nettie's been awful kind to us, lettin' us stay here with her.

CARRIE

Mr. Snow says a man that can't find work these days is jest bone lazy.

JULIE

Billy don't know any trade. He's only good at what he used to do. So now he jest don't do anythin'.

CARRIE

Wouldn't the carousel woman take him back?

JULIE

I think she would, but he won't go. I ask him why and he won't tell me . . . Last Monday he hit me.

CARRIE

Did you hit him back?

JULIE

No.

CARRIE

Whyn't you leave him?

JULIE

I don't want to.

CARRIE

I would. I'd leave him. Thinks he ken do whatever he likes jest because he's Billy Bigelow. Don't support you! Beats you! . . . He's a bad'n.

JULIE

He ain't willin'ly er meanin'ly bad.

CARRIE
(*Afraid she's hurting* JULIE)
Mebbe he ain't. That night you set on the bench together—he was gentle then, you told me.

JULIE

Yes, he was.

CARRIE

But now he's alw'ys actin' up—

JULIE

Not alw'ys. Sometimes he's gentle—even now. After supper, when he stands out here and listens to the music from the carousel— somethin' comes over him—and he's gentle.

CARRIE

What's he say?

JULIE

Nothin'. He jest sets and gets thoughtful. Y'see he's unhappy 'cause he ain't workin'. That's really why he hit me on Monday.

CARRIE

Fine reason fer hittin' you. Beats his wife 'cause he ain't workin'. (*She turns her head up left.* GIRLS, *caught eavesdropping, start to sweep vigorously.*)

JULIE

It preys on his mind.

CARRIE

Did he hurt you?

JULIE
(*Very eagerly*)

Oh, no—no.

CARRIE

Julie, I got some good news to tell you about me—about Mr. Snow and me. We're goin' to be cried in church nex' Sunday!

(*The* GIRLS *who have been upstage turn quickly, come down and cluster around* CARRIE, *proving they haven't missed a thing.* CARRIE *rises.*)

ALL GIRLS

What's thet you say, Carrie?
(*Ad libs of excitement*)
Carrie!
Honest and truly?
You fixin' t'get hitched?
Well, I never!
Do tell!

CARRIE

Jest a minute! Stop yer racket! Don't all come at me together!
(*But she is really pleased.*)

GIRL

Well, tell us! How long hev you been bespoke?

CARRIE

Near on t'two months. Julie was the fust t'know.

GIRL

What's he like, Julie?

CARRIE

Julie hes never see him. But you all will soon. He's comin' here.
I asked him to the clambake.

GIRL

Can't hardly wait'll I see him.

2ND GIRL

I can't hardly wait fer the weddin'.
(*All look at each other and giggle.*)

CARRIE
(*Giggling*)

Me neither.

JULIE

What a day that'll be fer you!

GIRLS
(*Singing*)

When you walk down the aisle
All the heads will turn.
What a rustlin' of bonnets there'll be!
And you'll try to smile,
But your cheeks will burn,
And your eyes'll get so dim you ken hardly see!

With your orange blossoms quiverin' in your hand,
You will stumble to the spot where the parson is.
Then your finger will be ringed with a gold band,
And you'll know the feller's yours—and you are his.

CARRIE

When I marry Mr. Snow—

GIRLS

What a day!
What a day!

CARRIE

The flowers'll be buzzin' with the hum of bees,

GIRLS

The birds'll make a racket in the churchyard trees,

CARRIE

When I marry Mr. Snow.

GIRLS

Heigh-ho!

CARRIE

Then it's off to home we'll go—

GIRLS

Spillin' rice
On the way!

CARRIE

And both of us'll look a little dreamy-eyed,
A-drivin' to a cottage by the oceanside
Where the salty breezes blow—
(SNOW *enters up left. He just couldn't be anyone else.*)

GIRLS

You and Mr. Snow!
(*Hearing his name,* MR. SNOW *preens.*)

CARRIE

He'll carry me cross the threshold,
And I'll be as meek as a lamb.
Then he'll set me on my feet

And I'll say, kinda sweet:
"Well, Mr. Snow, here I am!"
(*Now* MR. SNOW *is very pleased. He makes his presence known
by singing:*)

SNOW
Then I'll kiss her so she'll know,

CARRIE
(*Mortified*)
Mr. Snow!

GIRLS
(*Thrilled*)
Mr. Snow!

SNOW
That everythin'll be as right as right ken be,
A-livin' in a cottage by the sea with me,
Where the salty breezes blow!
(CARRIE *squeals and hides her head on* JULIE'*s shoulder. The*
GIRLS *are delighted.*)
I love Miss Pipp'ridge and I aim to
Make Miss Pipp'ridge change her name to
Missus Enoch Snow!

GIRLS
(*Ad lib*)
Carrie!
My lands, he give me sech a start!
Well! I never!

CARRIE
(*Looking up at* JULIE)
I'll neer look him in the face again! Never!
(*Laughs, shouts, whoops, and squeals from the* GIRLS.)

GIRL
C'mon inside and leave the two love-birds alone!
(*They exit into the house.* CARRIE *clings to* JULIE *and won't let her go.*)

CARRIE
(*Not turning to face him yet*)
Oh, Enoch!

SNOW
Surprised?

CARRIE
Surprised? I'm mortified!

SNOW
He-he!
(*This, we are afraid, is the way he laughs.* CARRIE *straightens out, looks at him, then beams back at* JULIE.)

CARRIE
Well, this is him.
(SNOW *bows and smiles. There is a moment of awkward silence.*)

JULIE
Carrie told me a lot about you.
(CARRIE *and* JULIE *nod to each other.* CARRIE *and* SNOW *nod.*)

CARRIE

I told you a lot about Julie, didn't I?
(CARRIE *and* SNOW *nod.* CARRIE *and* JULIE *nod.*)

JULIE

Carrie tells me you're comin' to the clambake.
(*He nods.*)

CARRIE

Looks like we'll hev good weather fer it, too.
(*They nod.*)

JULIE

Not a cloud in the sky.

SNOW

You're right.

CARRIE
(*To* JULIE)

He don't say much, but what he does say is awful pithy! (JULIE
nods. CARRIE *looks over toward her love. Still addressing* JULIE.) Is
he anythin' like I told you he was?

JULIE

Jest like.

SNOW

Oh, Carrie, I near fergot. I brought you some flowers.

CARRIE
(*Thrilled*)

Flowers? Where are they? (SNOW *hands her a small envelope from his inside pocket. She reads what is written on the package.*) Geranium seeds!

SNOW
(*Handing her another envelope*)
And this'n here is hydrangea. Thought we might plant 'em in front of the cottage. (*To* JULIE) They do good in the salt air.

JULIE
That'll be beautiful!

SNOW
I like diggin' around a garden in my spare time—Like t'plant flowers and take keer o' them. Does your husband like that too?

JULIE
N-no. I couldn't say right if Billy likes to take *keer* of flowers. He likes t'smell 'em, though.

CARRIE
Enoch's nice-lookin', ain't he?

SNOW
Oh come, Carrie!

CARRIE
Stiddy and reliable, too.—Well, ain't you goin' to wish us luck?

JULIE
(*Warmly*)
Of course I wish you luck, Carrie.
(JULIE *and* CARRIE *embrace.*)

CARRIE

You ken kiss Enoch, too—us bein' sech good friends, and me bein' right here lookin' on at you.
(JULIE *lets* ENOCH *kiss her on the cheek, which he shyly does. For a moment she clings to him, letting her head rest on his shoulder, as if it needed a shoulder very badly.* JULIE *starts to cry.*)

SNOW

Why are you crying, Mrs.—er—Mrs.—

CARRIE

It's because she has such a good heart.

SNOW

We thank you for your heartfelt sympathy. We thank you Mrs.—er—Mrs.—

JULIE

Mrs. Bigelow. Mrs. Billy Bigelow. That's my name—Mrs. B— (*She breaks off and starts to run into the house, but as she gets a little right of center,* BILLY *enters. He is followed by* JIGGER. JULIE *is embarrassed, recovers, and goes mechanically through the convention of introduction.*) Billy, you know Carrie. This is her intended— Mr. Snow.
(JIGGER *crosses up to the porch, standing under the arbor.*)

SNOW

Mr. Bigelow! I almost feel like I know you—

BILLY

How are you?
(*He starts up center.*)

SNOW

I'm pretty well. Jest getting' over a little chest cold. (As BILLY gets up center) This time of year—you know.
(*He stops, seeing that* BILLY *isn't listening.*)

JULIE

(*Turning to* BILLY)

Billy!

BILLY

(*He stops and turns to* JULIE, *crosses down to her in a defiant manner*)
Well, all right, say it. I stayed out all night—and I ain't workin'—and I'm livin' off yer Cousin Nettie.

JULIE

I didn't say anything.

BILLY

No, but it was on the tip of yer tongue!
(*He starts upstage center again.*)

JULIE

Billy! (*He turns*) Be sure and come back in time to go to the clambake.

BILLY

Ain't goin' to no clambake. Come on, Jigger.
(JIGGER, *who has been slinking upstage out of the picture, joins* BILLY *and they exit upstage center and off left.* JULIE *stands watching them, turns to* CARRIE, *then darts into the house to hide her humiliation.*)

CARRIE
(*To* SNOW, *after a pause*)
I'm glad you ain't got no whoop-jamboree notions like Billy.

SNOW
Well, Carrie, it alw'ys seemed t'me a man had enough to worry
about, getting' a good sleep o' nights so's to get in a good day's work
the next day, without goin' out an' lookin' fer any special trouble.

CARRIE
That's true, Enoch.

SNOW
A man's got to make plans fer his life—and then he's got to stick
to 'em.

CARRIE
Your plans are turnin' out fine, ain't they, Enoch?

SNOW
All accordin' to schedule, so far.
   (*Singing*)
   I own a little house,
   And a sail a little boat,
   And the fish I ketch I sell—
   And, in a manner of speakin',
   I'm doin' very well.

   I love a little girl
   And she's in love with me,
   And soon she'll be my bride
   And, in a manner of speakin',
   I should be satisfied.

CARRIE
(*Spoken*)

Well, ain't you?

SNOW

If I told you my plans, and the things I intend,
It'd make ev'ry curl on yer head stand on end!
  (*He takes her hand and becomes more intense, the gleam of
  ambition coming into his eye*)
When I make enough money outa one little boat,
I'll put all my money in another little boat.
I'll make twic't as much outa two little boats,
And the fust thing you know I'll hev four little boats!
Then eight little boats,
Then a fleet of little boats!
Then a great big fleet of great big boats!

All ketchin' herring,
Bringing it to shore,
Sailin' out again
And bringin' in more,
And more, and more,
And more!
  (*The music has become very operatic, rising in a crescendo far
  beyond what would ordinarily be justified by several boatloads
  of fish. But to this singer, boatloads of fish are kingdom come.*)

(*The following lines are spoken.*)

CARRIE

Who's goin' t'eat all thet herring?

SNOW

They ain't goin' to *be* herring! Goin' to put 'em in cans and call 'em sardines. Goin' to build a little sardine cannery—then a big one—then the biggest one in the country. Carrie, I'm goin' to get rich on sardines. I mean *we're* goin' t'get rich—you and me. I mean you and me—and—all of us.

(CARRIE *raises her eyes. Is the man bold enough to be meaning "children"?*)

(SNOW *sings:*)
The fust year we're married we'll hev one little kid,
The second year we'll go and hev another little kid,
You'll soon be darnin' socks fer eight little feet—

CARRIE
(*Enough is enough*)
Are you buildin' up to another fleet?

SNOW
(*Blissfully proceeding with his dream*)
We'll build a lot more rooms,
Our dear little house'll get bigger,
Our dear little house'll get bigger.

CARRIE
(*To herself*)
And so will my figger!

SNOW
(*Spoken*)
Carrie, ken y'imagine how it'll be when all the kids are upstairs in bed, and you and me sit alone by the fireside—me in my armchair, you on my knee—mebbe.

CARRIE

Mebbe.

(*And to his great delight,* CARRIE *sits on his knee. Both heave
a deep, contented sigh, and he starts to sing softly.*)

SNOW

When the children are asleep, we'll sit and dream
The things that ev'ry other
Dad and mother dream.
When the children are asleep and lights are low,
If I still love you the way
I love you today,
You'll pardon my saying: "I told you so!"
When the children are asleep, I'll dream with you.
We'll think: "What fun we have had!"
And be glad that it all came true.

CARRIE

When children are awake,
A-rompin' through the rooms
Or runnin' on the stairs,
Then, in a manner of speakin',
A house is really theirs.
But once they close their eyes
And we are left alone
And free from all their fuss,
Then, in a manner of speakin',
We ken be really us . . .

CARRIE

When the children are asleep
We'll sit and dream
The things that ev'ry other
Dad and mother dream—

Lo and behold!
If I still love you the way
I love you today,
You'll pardon my saying:
"I told you so!"

When the children are asleep,
I'll dream with you.
We'll think: "What fun we
    hev had!"
And be glad that it all came
    true.

You'll still hear me say
That the best dream I know
Is—When the children are
    asleep
I'll dream with you.

SNOW

Dream all alone,

Dreams that won't be
    interrupted
When the children are asleep
And lights are low.

You'll dream with me.

When today

Is a long time ago,
You'll still hear me say
That the best dream I know
Is you . . .

(*"Blow High, Blow Low" starts off stage.* SNOW *looks off left, then up right, takes* CARRIE's *chin in his hands and kisses her gently on the forehead. As the men enter singing, he looks up, takes his hat, which he left on the bait box. Then he and* CARRIE *exit.*)

MEN
(*Off stage, singing*)

Blow high, blow low!
A-whalin' we will go!
We'll go a-whalin', a-sailin' away,
Away we'll go,
Blow me high and low!

    (BILLY *and* JIGGER *enter, followed by friends from Jigger's whaler*)

For many and many a long, long day!
For many and many a long, long day!

    (*They sing another refrain. During this refrain* BILLY *looks toward the house. He is hesitant. Maybe he should go in to* JULIE. *He crosses to center.* JIGGER *sees this, crosses over to* BILLY.)

JIGGER

Hey, Billy! (BILLY *turns*) Where are you goin'? (BILLY *looks indecisive.* JIGGER *takes his arm and brings him downstage*) Stick with me. After we get rid of my shipmates, I wanna talk to you. Got an idea, for you and me to make money.

BILLY

How much?

JIGGER

More'n you ever saw in yer life.

MAN

Hey, Jigger, come back here!

    (BILLY *and* JIGGER *go back to the boys.* JIGGER *sings:*)

JIGGER

The people who live on land
Are hard to understand.
When you're lookin' for fun they clap you into jail!
So I'm shippin' off to sea,
Where life is gay and free,
And a feller can flip
A hook in the hip of a whale.

ALL

Blow high, blow low!
A-whalin' we will go!
We'll go a-whalin', a-sailin' away,
Away we'll go,
Blow me high and low!
For many and many a long, long day!
For many and many a long, long day!

BILLY

It's wonderful just to feel
Your hands upon a wheel
And to listen to wind a-whistlin' in a sail!
Or to climb aloft and be
The very first to see
A chrysanthemum spout come out o' the snout of a whale!

ALL

Blow high, blow low!
A-whalin' we will go!
We'll go a-whalin', a-sailin' away,
Away we'll go,
Blow me high and low!
For many and many a long, long day!

For many and many a long, long day!
(JIGGER *draws* BILLY *and the* MEN *around him. They crouch
low and* JIGGER *sings another verse.*)

JIGGER

A-rockin' upon the sea,
Your boat will seem to be
Like a dear little baby in her bassinet,
For she hasn't learned to walk,
And she hasn't learned to talk,
And her little behind
Is kind of inclined to be wet!
(*During the next refrain, more* SINGERS *come on, followed by*
DANCERS.)

ALL MEN

Blow high, blow low!
A-whalin' we will go!
We'll go a-whalin', a-sailin' away,
Away we'll go,
Blow me high and low!
For many and many a long, long day!
For many and many a long, long day!
(*Finish with big vocal climax.* JIGGER *takes* BILLY *off left, and
the* DANCERS *do:*)

Dance: Hornpipe.
(*At the finish of the number, all* DANCERS *clear the stage as*
BILLY *and* JIGGER *enter.*)

JIGGER

I tell you it's safe as sellin' cakes.

BILLY

You say this old sideburns who owns the mill is also the owner of your ship?

JIGGER

That's right. And tonight he'll be takin' three or four thousands dollars down to the captain—by hisself. He'll walk along the waterfront by hisself—with all that money.
(*He pauses to let this sink in.*)

BILLY

You'd think he'd have somebody go with him.

JIGGER

Not him! Not the last three times, anyway. I watched him from the same spot and see him pass me. Once I nearly jumped him.

BILLY

Why didn't you?

JIGGER

Don't like to do a job less it's air-tight. This one needs two to pull it off proper. Besides, there was a moon—shinin' on him like a torch. (*Spits*) Don't like moons. (*This is good news*) Lately the nights have been runnin' to fog. And it's ten to one we'll have fog tonight. That's why I wanted you to tell yer wife we'd go to that clambake.

BILLY

Clambake? Why?

JIGGER

Suppose we're over on the island and you and me get lost in the fog for a half an hour. And suppose we got in a boat and come over here and—and did whatever we had to do, and then go back? There's yer alibi! We just say we were lost on the island all that time.

BILLY

Just what would we have to do? I mean me. What would *I* have to do?

JIGGER

You go up to old sideburns and say: "Excuse me, sir. Could you tell me the time?"

BILLY

"Excuse me, sir. Could you tell me the time?" Then what?

JIGGER

Then? Well, by that time I got my knife in his ribs. Then you take *your* knife—

BILLY

Me? I ain't got a knife.

JIGGER

You can get one, can't you?

BILLY
(*After a pause, turning to* JIGGER)
Does he have to be killed?

JIGGER

No, he don't have to be. He can give up the money without bein' killed. But these New Englanders are funny. They'd rather be killed—Well?

BILLY

I won't do it. It's dirty.

JIGGER

What's dirty about it?

BILLY

The knife.

JIGGER

All right. Forget the knife. Just go up to him with a tin cup and say: "Please, sir, will you give me three thousand dollars?" See what he does fer you.

BILLY

I ain't goin' to do it.

JIGGER

Of course, if you got all the money you want, and don't need—

BILLY

I ain't got a cent. Money thinks I'm dead.
(MRS. MULLIN *is seen entering from up left, unnoticed by* BILLY *and* JIGGER.)

JIGGER

That's what I thought. And you're out of a job and you got a wife to support—

BILLY

Shut up about my wife. (*He sees* MRS. MULLIN) What do you want?

MRS. MULLIN

Hello, Billy.

BILLY

What did you come fer?

MRS. MULLIN

Come to talk business.

JIGGER

Business!
(*He spits.*)

MRS. MULLIN

I see you're still hangin' around yer jailbird friend.

BILLY

What's it to you who I hang around with?

JIGGER

If there's one thing I can't abide, it's the common type of woman.
(*He saunters upstage left and stands looking out to sea.*)

BILLY

What are you doin' here. You got a new barker, ain't you?

MRS. MULLIN
(*Looking him over*)
Whyn't you stay home and sleep at night? You look awful!

BILLY

He's as good as me, ain't he?

MRS. MULLIN
Push yer hair back off yer forehead—

BILLY
(*Pushing her hand away and turning away from her*)
Let my hair be.

MRS. MULLIN
If I told you to let it hang down over yer eyes you'd push it back.
I hear you been beatin' her. If you're sick of her, why don't you
leave her? No use beatin' the poor, skinny little—

BILLY
Leave her, eh? You'd like that, wouldn't you?

MRS. MULLIN
Don't flatter yourself! (*Her pride stung, she paces to center stage*)
If I had any sense I wouldn' of come here. The things you got
to do when you're in business! . . . I'd sell the damn carousel if
I could.

BILLY
Ain't it crowded without me?

MRS. MULLIN
Those fool girls keep askin' for you. They miss you, see? Are you
goin' to be sensible and come back?

BILLY
And leave Julie?

MRS. MULLIN
You beat her, don't you?

BILLY
(*Exasperated*)
No, I don't beat her. What's all this damn-fool talk about
beatin'? I hit her once, and now the whole town is—the next
one I hear—I'll smash—

MRS. MULLIN
(*Backing away from him*)
All right! All right! I take it back. I don't want to get mixed up
in it.

BILLY
Beatin' her! As if I'd beat her!

MRS. MULLIN
What's the odds one way er another? Looks at the thing straight.
You been married two months and you're sick of it. Out there's
the carousel. Show booths, young girls, all the beer you want, a
good livin'—and you're throwin' it all away. Know what? I got a
new organ.

BILLY
I know.

MRS. MULLIN
How do you know?

BILLY
(*His voice softer*)
You can hear it from here. I listen to it every night.

MRS. MULLIN
Good one, ain't it?

BILLY

Jim dandy. Got a nice tone.

MRS. MULLIN

Y'ought to come up close and hear it. Makes you think the carousel is goin' faster . . . You belong out there and you know it. You ain't cut out fer a respectable married man. You're an artist type. You belong among artists. Tell you what: you come back and I'll give you a ruby ring my husband left me.

BILLY

I dunno—I might go back. I could still go on livin' here with Julie.

MRS. MULLIN

Holy Moses!

BILLY

What's wrong?

MRS. MULLIN

Can y'imagine how the girls'd love that? A barker who runs home to his wife every night! Why, people'd laugh theirselves sick.

BILLY

I know what *you* want.

MRS. MULLIN

Don't be so stuck on yerself.

BILLY

I ain't happy here, and *that's* the truth.

MRS. MULLIN

Course you ain't.

(*She strokes his hair back off his forehead, and this time he lets her.* JULIE *enters from house, carrying a tray with a cup of coffee and a plate of cakes on it.* MRS. MULLIN *pulls her hand away. There is a slight pause.*)

BILLY

Do you want anythin'?

JULIE

I brought you your coffee.

MRS. MULLIN
(*To* BILLY *in a low voice*)
Whyn't you have a talk with her? She'll understand. Maybe she'll be glad to get rid of you.

BILLY
(*Without conviction*)

Maybe.

JULIE

Billy—before I ferget. I got somethin' to tell you.

BILLY

All right.

JULIE

I been wantin' to tell you—in fact, I was goin' to yesterday.

BILLY

Well, go ahead.

JULIE

I can't—we got to be alone.

BILLY

Don't you see I'm busy? Here, I'm talkin' business and—

JULIE

It'll only take a minute.

BILLY

Get out o' here, or—

JULIE

I tell you it'll only take a minute.

BILLY

Will you get out of here?

JULIE

No.

BILLY

What did you say?

MRS. MULLIN

Let her alone, Billy. I'll drop in at Bascombe's bank and get some small change for the carousel. I'll be back in a few minutes for your answer to my proposition.

(*Exits above* JIGGER. *She looks at* JIGGER *as she goes.* JIGGER *looks at* BILLY, *then follows* MRS. MULLIN *off.*)

JULIE

Don't look at me like that. I ain't afraid of you—ain't afraid of anyone. I hev somethin' to tell you.

BILLY

Well then, tell me, and make it quick.

JULIE

I can't tell it so quick. Why don't you drink yer coffee?

BILLY

That what you wanted to tell me?

JULIE

No. By the time you drink it, I'll hev told you.

BILLY
(*Stirs coffee and takes a quick sip*)

Well?

JULIE

Yesterday my head ached and you asked me—

BILLY

Yes—

JULIE

Well—you see—thet's what it is.

BILLY

You sick?

JULIE

No. It's nothin' like thet. (*He puts cup down*) It's awful hard to tell you—I'm not a bit skeered, because it's a perfectly natural thing—

BILLY

What is?

JULIE

Well—when two people live together—

BILLY

Yes—

JULIE

I'm goin' to hev a baby.
(*She turns away. He sits still and stunned. Then he rises, crosses to her, and puts his arms around her. She leans her head back on his shoulders. Then she leaves and starts for the house. As she gets to the steps,* BILLY *runs and helps her very solicitously.* JIGGER *has re-entered and calls to* BILLY.)

JIGGER
(*Two short whistles*)

Hey, Billy!

BILLY
(*Turning to* JIGGER)

Hey, Jigger! Julie—Julie's goin' to have a baby.

JIGGER
(*Calmly smoking his cigarette*)

Yeh? What about it?

(*Disgusted at* JIGGER)

Nothin'.
(*He goes into the house.*)

JIGGER
(*Ruminating*)

My mother had a baby once.
(*He smiles angelically and puffs on his cigarette.* MRS. MULLIN *enters.*)

MRS. MULLIN

He in there with her? (JIGGER *ignores the question*) They're havin' it out, I bet. (JIGGER *impudently blows a puff of smoke in her direction*) When he comes back to me I ain't goin' to let him hang around with you any more. You know that, don't you?

JIGGER

Common woman.

MRS. MULLIN

Ain't goin' to let him get in your clutches. Everybody that gets mixed up with you finishes in the jailhouse—or the grave.

JIGGER

Tut-tut-t-t-t-. Carnival blonde! Comin' between a man and his wife!

MRS. MULLIN

Comin' between nothin'! They don't belong together. Nobody knows him like I do. And nobody is goin' to get him away from me. And that goes fer you!

JIGGER

Who wants him? If he's goin' to let himself get tied up to an old wobbly-hipped slut like you, what good would he be to me?

MRS. MULLIN

He won't be *no* good to you! And he won't end up with a perliceman's bullet in his heart—like that Roberts boy you hung around with last year. Wisht the bullet hadda got you—you sleek-eyed wharf rat! You keep away from him that's all, or I'll get the cops after you.

JIGGER
(*Holding his cigarette high*)
Common woman!

MRS. MULLIN

Yeh! Call names! But I got him back just the same! And you're through!

JIGGER

Put on a new coat o' paint. You're starting to peel! Old pleasure boat!
(*He exits. She looks off after him, then turns right and sees* BILLY *coming out of the house. She immediately shifts all her attention to the essential job of holding his interest. She primps and walks center. He comes down by bait box.*)

BILLY
(*A change has come over him. There is a strange, firm dignity in his manner*)
You still here?
(*He picks up tray, and sits on box, tray in his lap.*)

MRS. MULLIN

Didn't you tell me to come back? (*Taking money out of dress*) Here! You'll be wantin' an advance on yer salary. Well, that's only fair. You been out o' work a long time. (*She offers him money.*)

BILLY

(*Taking another sip of coffee*)

Go home, Mrs. Mullin.

MRS. MULLIN

What's the matter with you?

BILLY

Can't you see I'm havin' my breakfast? Go back to your carousel.

MRS. MULLIN

You mean you ain't comin' with me?

BILLY

(*Still holding cup*)

Get out of here. Get!

MRS. MULLIN

I'll never speak to you again—not if you were dyin', I wouldn't.

BILLY

That worries me a lot.

MRS. MULLIN

What did she tell you in there?

BILLY
(*Putting cup on tray*)

She told me—

MRS. MULLIN

Some lies about me, I bet!

BILLY
(*Proudly*)

No, Mrs. Mullin. Nothin' about you. Just about Julie and me—
and—(*Looking up at her*) As a matter of fact, Mrs. Mullin—I'm
goin' to be a father!

MRS. MULLIN

You!—Julie!—?

BILLY

Good-by, Mrs. Mullin.

MRS. MULLIN

You a father?
(*She starts to laugh.*)

BILLY
(*Giving her a good push*)

Get the hell away from here, Mrs. Mullin. (*She continues to
laugh*) Good-by, Mrs. Mullin!
(*He pushes her again, and as she reaches the left portal, he
gives her a good kick in the bustle. Then he turns, looks toward
Nettie's house, smiles. He starts to contemplate the future. He
starts to sing softly.*)
I wonder what he'll think of me!
I guess he'll call me

"The old man."
I guess he'll think I can lick
Ev'ry other feller's father—
Well, I can!
   (*He gives his belt a hitch*)
I bet that he'll turn out to be
The spit an' image
Of his dad.
But he'll have more common sense
Than his puddin'-headed father
Ever had.
I'll teach him to wrassle
And dive through a wave,
When we go in the mornin's for our swim.
His mother can teach him
The way to behave,
But she won't make a sissy out o' him—
Not him!
Not my boy!
Not Bill . . .
   (*The name, coming to his lips involuntarily, pleases him very much*)
Bill!
   (*He loves saying it. He straightens up proudly*)
My boy, Bill!
(I will see
that he's named
After me,
I will!)
My boy, Bill—
He'll be tall
And as tough
As a tree,

Will Bill!
Like a tree he'll grow
With his head held high
And his feet planted firm on the ground,
And you won't see no-
body dare to try
To boss him or toss him around!
No pot-bellied, baggy-eyed bully'll boss him around!
(*Having worked himself up to a high pitch of indignation, he
relaxes into a more philosophical manner*)
I don't give a damn what he does,
As long as he does what he likes.
He can sit on his tail
Or work on a rail
With a hammer, a-hammerin' spikes.

He can ferry a boat on the river
Or peddle a pack on his back
Or work up and down
The streets of a town
With a whip and a horse and a hack.

He can haul a scow along a canal,
Run a cow around a corral,
Or maybe bark for a carousel—
(*This worries him*)
Of course it takes talent to do *that* well.

He might be a champ of the heavyweights
Or a feller that sells you glue,
Or President of the United States—
That'd be all right, too.

Jean Darling, John Raitt, and Jan Clayton in the original Broadway production, 1945.

The graduation scene ("You'll Never Walk Alone") in the original Broadway production, 1945.

Set design rendering by Jo Mielziner for the original 1945 Broadway production.

The prelude ("The Carousel Waltz") from the original Broadway production, 1945.

The film version, 1956.

Gordan MacRae and Shirley Jones in the film version, 1956.

A BEAUTIFUL INDIGO BLUE

Early in June 1992, Nick Hytner and I traveled to New England to research our production of Carousel.

Whilst driving up the coast of Maine, we came across one of the last remaining Shaker communities in America, Sabbathday Lake. They showed us into their original Meeting House, built in the early 1800s. Inside, the walls were painted a beautiful indigo blue to symbolize Heaven.

From that small, blue New England room where the Shakers used to congregate to pray, sing and dance, grew the image of the empty blue box with the revolving floor which is now the essence of the current design and in which our cast now congregates to sing and dance.

—Bob Crowley, Designer

Royal National Theatre production, London 1993. Note by scenery and costume designer Bob Crowley.

"The Carousel Waltz"—Royal National Theatre production at Lincoln Center Theater, 1994.

Audra Ann McDonald, Michael Hayden, and Sally Murphy, 1994 Lincoln Center Theater production.

1994 Lincoln Center Theater production.

Jon Marshall Sharp and Sandra Brown, 1994 Lincoln Center Theater production.

Stephanie Blythe and company in "A Real Nice Clambake"—*Carousel in Concert*, New York Philharmonic at Avery Fisher Hall, 2013.

Lauren Lovette and Robert Fairchild perform in "Carousel (A Dance)"—choreographed by Christopher Wheeldon, New York City Ballet, for the Richard Rodgers Centennial in 2002. Photo from a 2013 performance.

Notes by Oscar Hammerstein II for Billy's speech to Julie in the graduation scene.

Laura Osnes and Steven Pasquale, Lyric Opera of Chicago, 2015.

"Blow High, Blow Low"—Lyric Opera of Chicago, 2015.

(*Orchestra picks up the theme of "My boy, Bill."* BILLY *speaks over music*)

His mother'd like that. But he wouldn't be President unless he wanted to be!

(*Singing*)
Not Bill!
My boy, Bill—
He'll be tall
And as tough
As a tree,
Will Bill!

Like a tree he'll grow,
With his head held high,
And his feet planted firm on the ground,
And you won't see no-
body dare to try
To boss him or toss him around!
No flat-bottomed, flabby-faced, pot-bellied, baggy-eyed
    bastard'll boss him around!
(*He paces the stage angrily*)
And I'm damned if he'll marry his boss's daughter,
A skinny-lipped virgin with blood like water,
Who'll give him a peck and call it a kiss
And look in his eyes through a lorgnette—
Say!
Why am I carryin' on like this?
My kid ain't even been born yet!
(*He laughs loudly at himself, crosses up to bait box, and sits.
Then he returns to more agreeable daydreaming*)
I can see him
When he's seventeen or so

And startin' in to go
With a girl.

I can give him
Lots o' pointers, very sound,
On the way to get round
Any girl.

I can tell him—
Wait a minute! Could it be—?
What the hell! What if he
Is a girl!
>   (*Rises in anguish*)
Bill!
Oh, Bill!
>   (*He sits on a bait box and holds his head in his hands. The
>   music becomes the original theme, "I Wonder What He'll
>   Think of Me." He speaks over it in a moaning voice*)

What would I do with her? What could I do for her? A bum—
with no money!
>   (*Singing the last lines of the first stanza*)
You can have fun with a son,
But you got to be a *father*
To a girl!
>   (*Thinking it over, he begins to be reconciled*)
She mightn't be so bad at that—
A kid with ribbons
In her hair,
A kind o' neat and petit
Little tintype of her mother—
What a pair!
>   (*Warming up to the idea, speaking over music*)
I can just hear myself braggin' about her!

(*Singing*)
My little girl,
Pink and white
As peaches and cream is she.
My little girl
Is half again as bright
As girls are meant to be!
Dozens of boys pursue her,
Many a likely lad
Does what he can to woo her
From her faithful dad.
She has a few
Pink and white young fellers of two or three—
But my little girl
Gets hungry ev'ry night
And she comes home to me!
My little girl!
   (*More thoughtful, and serious*)
My little girl!
   (*Suddenly panicky*)
I got to get ready before she comes!
I got to make certain that she
Won't be dragged up in slums
With a lot o' bums—
Like me!

She's got to be sheltered and fed, and dressed
In the best that money can buy!
I never knew how to get money,
But I'll try—
By God! I'll try!
I'll go out and make it
Or steal it or take it

Or die!

(*Finishing, he stands still and thoughtful. Then he turns right and walks slowly up to the bait box and gazes off right. As he does,* NETTIE *comes out of the house, carrying a large jug. She crosses up center and puts the jug on the steps left center, then calls off.*)

NETTIE

Hey, you roustabouts! Time to get goin'! Come and help us carry everythin' on the boats!

MAN
(*Off*)

All right, Nettie, we're comin'!

2ND MAN

Don't need to hev a fit about it.

NETTIE

Hey, Billy! What's this Julie says about you not goin' to the clambake?

BILLY

Clambake? (*Suddenly getting an idea from the word*) Mebbe I *will* go, after all! (*General laughter off stage.* JIGGER *enters down left.* BILLY *sees him. To* NETTIE.) There's Jigger. I got to talk to him. Jigger! Hey, Jigger! Come here—quick!

NETTIE

I'll tell Julie you're comin'. She'll be tickled pink.
(*She goes into the house.*)

BILLY

Jigger, I changed my mind! You now—about goin' to the clam-bake, and—I'll do everythin' like you said. Gotta get money on account of the baby, see.

JIGGER

Sure, the baby. (*He pulls* BILLY *closer and lowers his voice*) Did you get the knife?

BILLY

Knife?

JIGGER

I only got a pocket knife. If he shows fight we'll need a real one.

BILLY

But I ain't got—

JIGGER

Go inside and take the kitchen knife.

BILLY

Somebody might see me.

JIGGER

Take it so they don't see you!
(BILLY *looks indecisive.* JULIE *enters on the run to* BILLY *from the house.*)

JULIE

Billy, is it true? Are you comin'?

BILLY

I think so. Yes.

JULIE

(*Puts her arm around his waist. He puts his arms
around her*)
We'll hev a barrel of fun. I'll show you all over the island. Know
every inch of it. Been goin' to picnics there since I been a little
girl.

JIGGER

Billy! Billy! Y'better go and get that—

JULIE

Get what, Billy?

BILLY

Why—

JIGGER

The shawl. Billy said you oughter have a shawl. Gets cold at
nights. Fog comes up—ain't that what you said?
    (*People start entering with baskets, pies, jugs, etc., ready to go
    to the clambake.*)

BILLY

Y-yes. I better go and get it—the shawl.

JULIE

Now, that was real thoughtful, Billy.
    (*We see* NETTIE *coming out of the house. The stage is pretty
    well crowded by now.*)

BILLY

I'll go and get it.

(*He exits into the house quickly.*)

NETTIE

C'mon, all!

(*From the house come* GIRLS *carrying cakes, pies, butter crocks; men carrying baskets.* NETTIE *sings*)
June is bustin' out all over!

ALL

The flowers are bustin' from their seed!

NETTIE

And the pleasant life of Riley
That is spoken of so highly
Is the life that ev'rybody wants to lead!

ALL

Because it's June!
June—June—June!
Jest because it's June—June—June!

(*During this singing chorus,* SNOW *and* CARRIE *have entered from the house.* JULIE *is seen running over to* CARRIE *to tell her the good news that* BILLY *is going to the clambake.* JIGGER *crosses to* JULIE *and is introduced to* CARRIE. JIGGER *looks her over.* JULIE *also introduces* JIGGER *to* SNOW, *but* JIGGER *just brushes him off.* SNOW *tries to smile; but misses by a good margin. On the last "June" of the refrain, everyone but* JULIE *and* JIGGER *exit.* BILLY *comes out of the house carrying the shawl. He crosses to* JULIE, *who is now a little left of center and downstage.* JIGGER *is right stage. As* BILLY *is putting the shawl over* JULIE'*s shoulder,* JIGGER *works his way over to*

BILLY *as if to say, "Did you get the knife?"* BILLY *pantomimes that it's in the inside pocket of his vest.* JULIE *turns in time to see this.* BILLY *quickly takes her arm and walks her off.* JIGGER *has his pocket knife in his hand and is testing the sharpness of the blade and is following* BILLY *off as*

THE CURTAIN FALLS.

ACT 2

Scene 1

SCENE: *On an island across the bay. That night.*
The backdrop depicts the bay, seen between two sand dunes.

AT RISE: *It is too dark to define the characters until a moment after the rise of the curtain when the lights start a gradual "dim-up" as if a cloud were unveiling the moon. Down left* BILLY *is seen lying stretched at full length, his head on* JULIE*'s lap. There is a small group right center dominated by* NETTIE, SNOW, *and* CARRIE. *Upstage several couples recline in chosen isolation at the edge of the trees.*
The mood of the scene is the languorous contentment that comes to people who have just had a good meal in the open air.
The curtain is up several seconds before the first speech is heard.

NETTIE
(*After a loud sigh*)
Dunno as I should hev et those last four dozen clams!

GIRL
Look here, Orrin Peasely! You jest keep your hands in yer pockets if they're so cold.

ALL
(*Softly*)
This was a real nice clambake,
We're mighty glad we came.
The vittles we et
Were good, you bet!

The company was the same.
Our hearts are warm,
Our bellies are full,
And we are feelin' prime.
This was a real nice clambake
And we all had a real good time!

NETTIE

Fust come codfish chowder,
Cooked in iron kettles,
Onions floatin' on the top,
Curlin' up in petals!

JULIE

Throwed in ribbons of salted pork.

ALL

An old New England trick.

JULIE

And lapped it all up with a clamshell,
Tied on to a bayberry stick!

ALL

Oh-h-h—
This was a real nice clambake,
We're mighty glad we came.
The vittles we et
Were good, you bet!
The company was the same.
Our hearts are warm,
Our bellies are full,
And we are feelin' prime.

This was a real nice clambake
And we all had a real good time!
(*The memory of the delectable feast restores* SNOW'*s spirit and*
he rises and crosses to center and sings very soulfully:)

SNOW

Remember when we raked
Them red-hot lobsters
Out of the driftwood fire?
They sizzled and crackled
And sputtered a song,
Fitten for an angels' choir.

ALL GIRLS

Fitten fer an angels',
Fitten fer an angels',
Fitten fer an angels' choir!

NETTIE

We slit 'em down the back
And peppered 'em good,
And doused 'em in melted butter—

CARRIE
(*Savagely*)

Then we tore away the claws
And cracked 'em with our teeth
'Cause we weren't in the mood to putter!

ALL

Fitten fer an angels',
Fitten fer an angels',
Fitten fer an angels' choir!

MAN
Then at last come the clams—

ALL
Steamed under rockweed
And poppin' from their shells,
Jest how many of 'em
Galloped down our gullets—
We couldn't say oursel's!
Oh-h-h-h-h—
This was a real nice clambake,
We're mighty glad we came!
The vittles we et
Were good, you bet!
The company was the same.
Our hearts are warm,
Our bellies are full,
And we are feelin' prime.
This was a real nice clambake,
And we all had a real good time!

We said it afore—
And we'll say it agen—
We all had a real good time!

CARRIE
Hey, Nettie! Ain't it 'bout time the boys started their treasure-hunt?

MEN
(*Ad lib*)
Sure!
Feel like I'm goin' to win it this year.

Let's get goin'.

NETTIE

Jest a minute! Nobody's goin' treasure-huntin' till we get this island cleaned up. Can't leave it like this fer the next picnickers that come.

ALL MEN

Ah, Nettie—

NETTIE

Bogue in and get to work! The whole kit and kaboodle of you! Burn that rubbish! Gather up those bottles!

ALL MEN AND WOMEN
(*Ad libs*)

All right, all right.
Needn't hev a catnip fit!
(JULIE *exits. All start to leave the stage in all directions.*)

NETTIE

Hey, Enoch! While they're cleanin' up, you go hide the treasure.
(*She exits.*)

JIGGER

Why should *he* get out of workin'?

CARRIE
(*Proudly*)

'Cause he found the treasure last year. One that finds it hides it the next year. That's the way we do!
(CARRIE *and* SNOW *cross upstage of* BILLY *and* JIGGER *and exit.* JIGGER *starts to follow.*)

BILLY

Hey, Jigger!

JIGGER
(*Looking off after* CARRIE)
That's a well-set-up little piece, that Carrie.

BILLY

Ain't it near time fer us to start?

JIGGER

No. We'll wait till they're ready fer that treasure-hunt. That'll be a good way fer you and me to leave. We'll be a team, see? Then we'll get lost together like I said. (BILLY *is moving about nervously)* Stop jumping from one foot to the other. Go along to yer wife—and tell that little Carrie to come and talk to me.

BILLY

Look, Jigger, you ain't got time fer girls tonight.

JIGGER

Sure I have. You know me—quick or nothin'!

BILLY

Jigger—after we do it—what do we do then?

JIGGER

Bury the money—and go on like nothin' happened for six months. Wait another six months and then buy passage on a ship.

BILLY

The baby'll be born by then.

JIGGER

We'll take it along with us.

BILLY

Maybe we'll sail to San Francisco.

JIGGER

Why do you keep puttin' yer hand on yer chest?

BILLY

My heart's bumpin' up and down under the knife.

JIGGER

Put the knife on the other side.
(CARRIE *enters.*)

CARRIE

Mr. Bigelow, Julie says you should come and help her. (BILLY
exits. CARRIE *turns to* JIGGER) Why ain't *you* workin'?

JIGGER

I don't feel so well.

CARRIE

It's mebbe the clams not settin' so good on yer stummick.

JIGGER

Nope. It's nothin' on my stummick. It's somethin' on my mind.
(*He takes* CARRIE's *arm*) Sit down here with me a minute. I want
yer advice.

CARRIE

(*Sitting on an upturned basket*)

Now, look here, Mr. Craigin, I ain't got no time fer no wharf yarns or spoondrift.

JIGGER
(*Squashing out his cigarette*)
I want yer advice. (*Suddenly throws his arms around her*) You're sweeter than sugar and I'm crazy fer you. Never had this feelin' before fer anyone—

CARRIE
Mr. Craigin!

JIGGER
Ain't nothin' I wouldn't do fer you. Why, jest to see yer lovely smile—I'd swim through beer with my mouth closed. You're the only girl fer me. How about a little kiss?

CARRIE
Mr. Craigin, I couldn't.

JIGGER
Didn't you hear me say I loved you?

CARRIE
I'm awful sorry fer you, but what can I do? Enoch and me are goin' to be cried in church next Sunday.

JIGGER
Next Sunday I'll be far out at sea lookin' at the icy gray water. Mebbe I'll jump in and drown myself!

CARRIE
Oh, don't!

JIGGER

Well, then, give me a kiss. (*Grabbing her arm. Good and sore now*)
One measly little kiss!

CARRIE

(*Pushing his arm away*)
Enoch wouldn't like it.

JIGGER

I don't wanta kiss Enoch.

CARRIE

(*Drawing herself up resolutely*)
I'll thank you not to yell at me, Mr. Craigin. If you love me like
you say you do, then please show me the same respect like you
would if you didn't love me.
(*She starts to stalk off left.* JIGGER *is a stayer and not easily
shaken off. He decides to try one more method. It worked once
long ago on a girl in Liverpool.*)

JIGGER

(*In despair*)
Carrie! (*She stops; he crosses to her*) Miss Pipperidge! Just one
word, please. (*He becomes quite humble*) I know I don't deserve
yer fergiveness. Only, I couldn't help myself. Fer a few awful
minutes I—I let the brute come out in me.

CARRIE

I think I understand, Mr. Craigin.

JIGGER

Thank you, Miss Pipperidge, thank you kindly. There's just one
thing that worries me and it worries me a lot—it's about you.

CARRIE

About me?

JIGGER

You're such a little innercent. You had no right to stay here alone and talk with a man you hardly knew. Suppose I was a different type of feller—you know, unprincipled—a feller who'd use his physical strength to have his will—there are such men, you know.

CARRIE

I know, but—

JIGGER

Every girl ought to know how to defend herself against beasts like that. (*Proceeding slyly up to his point*) Now, there are certain grips in wrestlin' I could teach you—tricks that'll land a masher flat on his face in two minutes.

CARRIE

But I ain't strong enough—

JIGGER

It don't take strength—it's all in balance—a twist of the wrist and a dig with the elbow—Here, just let me show you a simple one. This might save yer life some day. Suppose a feller grabs you like this. (*Puts both arms around her waist*) Now you put yer two hands on my neck. (*She does*) Now pull me toward you. (*She does*) That's it. Now pull my head down. Good! Now put yer left arm all the way around my neck. Now squeeze—hard! Tighter! (*Slides his right hand down her back and pats her bustle*) Good girl!

CARRIE

(*Holding him tight*)

Does it hurt?

JIGGER

(*Having the time of his life*)

You got me helpless!

CARRIE

Show me another one!
(*She lets him go.*)

JIGGER

Right! Here's how you can pick a feller up and send him sprawl-lin'. Now I'll stand here, and you get hold of—Wait a minute. I'll do it to you first. Then you can do it to me. Stand still and relax. (*He takes her hand and foot and slings her quickly over his shoulders*) This is the way firemen carry people.

CARRIE

(*A little breathless and stunned*)

Is it?

JIGGER

See how helpless you can make a feller if he gets fresh with you?
(*He starts to walk off with her*)

CARRIE

Mr. Craig—(S*he stops, because* something *terrible has happened.* SNOW *has entered.* JIGGER *sees him and stops, still holding* CARRIE *over his shoulders, fireman style. After a terrifying pause,* CARRIE *speaks:*) Hello, Enoch. (*No answer*) This is the way firemen carry people.

SNOW
(*Grimly*)
Where's the fire?

(JIGGER *puts her down between* SNOW *and himself.*)

CARRIE
(*Crossing to* SNOW)
He was only showin' me how to defend myself.

SNOW
It didn't look like you had learned very much by the time I came!

JIGGER
Oh, what's all the fussin' and fuzzlin' and wuzzlin' about?

SNOW
In my opinion, sir, you are as scurvy a hunk o' scum as I ever see near the water's edge at low tide!

JIGGER
(*Turning his profile to* SNOW)
The same—side view!

SNOW
I—I never thought I'd see the woman I am engaged to bein' carried out o' the woods like a fallen deer!

CARRIE
He wasn't carryin' me out o' the woods. He was carryin' me *into* the woods. No, I don't mean that!

SNOW

I think we hev said all we hev to say. I can't abide women who are free, loose, and lallygaggin'—and I certainly would never marry one!

CARRIE

But, Enoch!

SNOW

Leave me, please. Leave me alone with my shattered dreams. They are all I hev left—memories of what didn't happen! (CARRIE *turns upstage and crosses to* JIGGER. *He puts his arms around her. She starts to whimper.* SNOW *looks out into space with pained eyes, and sings:*)
> Geraniums in the winder,
> Hydrangeas on the lawn,
> And breakfast in the kitchen
> In the timid pink of dawn,
> And you to blow me kisses
> When I headed fer the sea—
> We might hev been
> A happy pair
> Of lovers—
> Mightn't hev we?
> (*Another sob from* CARRIE. SNOW *continues:*)
> And comin' home at twilight,
> It might hev been so sweet
> To take my ketch of herring
> And lay them at your feet!
> (*Swallowing hard*)
> I might hev hed a baby—

JIGGER

What!

SNOW

(*Glares at* JIGGER, *then out front again*)
To dandle on my knee,
But all these things
That might hev been
Are never,
Never to be!
(*At this point* CARRIE *just lets loose and bawls, and buries her head in* JIGGER's *shoulder. Some people hear this and enter as* JIGGER *consoles her.*)

JIGGER

I never see it yet to fail,
I never see it fail!
A girl who's in love with a virtuous man
Is doomed to weep and wail.
(*More people enter and get into the scene*)
Stonecutters cut it on stone,
Woodpeckers peck it on wood:
There's nothin' so bad fer a woman
As a man who thinks he's good!
(CARRIE *bawls out one loud note. More people enter.*)

SNOW

Nice talk!

JIGGER

My mother used to say to me:
"When you grow up, my son,

I hope you're a bum like yer father was,
'Cause a good man ain't no fun."

JIGGER AND CHORUS

Stonecutters cut it on stone,
Woodpeckers peck it on wood:
There's nothin' so bad fer a woman
As a man who thinks he's good!
(*From here on, the* CHORUS *takes sides.*)

SNOW

'Tain't so!

JIGGER

'Tis too!

SNOW'S CHORUS

'Tain't so!

JIGGER'S CHORUS

'Tis too!
(SNOW *crosses to right, followed by Carrie*)

CARRIE

Enoch—Say you forgive me! Say somethin' sweet to me, Enoch—
somethin' soft and sweet. (*He remains silent and she becomes
exasperated*) Say somethin' soft and sweet!

SNOW
(*Turning to* CARRIE, *fiercely*)
Boston cream pie!
(*Turns and exits.* CARRIE *cries.* BILLY *enters and crosses to*
JIGGER.)

BILLY

Hey, Jigger—don't you think?

JIGGER

Huh? (*Catches on, raises his voice to all*) When are we goin' to start
that treasure-hunt?

NETTIE

Right now! Y'all got yer partners? Two men to each team. You
got half an hour to find the treasure. The winners can kiss any
girls they want!
(*A whoop and a holler goes up and all the men and the dancing
girls start out.* JULIE *enters from down left and sees* BILLY
starting out with JIGGER.)

JULIE

Billy—are you goin' with Jigger? Don't you think that's foolish?

BILLY

Why?

JULIE

Neither one of you knows the island good. You ought to split
up and each go with—

BILLY
(*Brushing her aside*)
We're partners, see? C'mon, Jigger.

CARRIE

I don't know what gets into men. Enoch put on a new suit today
and he was a different person.
(*They all group around* JULIE.)

GIRL
(*Singing*)

I never see it yet to fail.

ALL GIRLS

I never see it fail.
A girl who's in love with any man
Is doomed to weep and wail.

1ST GIRL
(*Spoken*)

And it's even worse after they marry you.

2ND GIRL

You ought to give him back that ring, Carrie. You'd be better off.

3RD GIRL

Here's Arminy—been married a year. She'll tell you.

ARMINY
(*Singing with a feeling of futility*)

The clock jest ticks yer life away,
There's no relief in sight.
It's cookin' and scrubbin' and sewin' all day
And Gawd-knows-whatin' all night!

ALL

Stonecutters cut it on stone,
Woodpeckers peck it on wood:
There's nothin' so bad fer a woman
As a man who's bad or good!

CARRIE
(*Spoken*)

It makes you wonder, don't it?

GIRL

Now you tell her, Julie.

2ND GIRL

She's your best girl friend.

ALL GIRLS
(*Singing*)

Tell it to her good, Julie,
Tell it to her good!

(JULIE *smiles. The* GIRLS *group around her expectantly.* JULIE
starts singing softly and earnestly to CARRIE, *but as she goes on,
she quite obviously becomes autobiographical in her philosophy.
Her singing is quiet, almost recited. The orchestration is light.
The* GIRLS *hold the picture, perfectly still, like figures in a
painting.*)

JULIE
(*Singing*)

What's the use of wond'rin'
If he's good or if he's bad,
Or if you like the way he wears his hat?
Oh, what's the use of wond'rin'
If he's good or if he's bad?
He's your feller and you love him—
That's all there is to that.

Common sense may tell you
That the endin' will be sad

And now's the time to break and run away.
But what's the use of wond'rin'
If the endin' will be sad?
He's your feller and you love him—
There's nothin' more to say.

Somethin' made him the way that he is,
Whether he's false or true.
And somethin' gave him the things that are his—
One of those things is you.

So
When he wants your kisses
You will give them to the lad,
And anywhere he leads you, you will walk.
And anytime he needs you,
You'll go runnin' there like mad!
You're his girl and he's your feller—
And the rest is all talk.

> (*As* JULIE *finishes her song, we see* BILLY *and* JIGGER *entering, crouching behind the sand dunes.* JULIE *turns just in time to see them as they get up center.* JULIE *crosses to* BILLY.)

JULIE

Billy! Billy! Where you goin'?

BILLY

Where we goin'?

JIGGER

We're looking for the treasure.

JULIE

I don't want you to, Billy. Let me come with you.

JIGGER

No.

JULIE

(*Putting her hands to his chest and feeling the knife*)
Billy!

BILLY

I got no time to fool with women. Get out of my way!
(*He succeeds in shoving her aside.*)

JULIE

Let me have that. Oh, Billy. Please—
(*He exits.* JIGGER *follows.* NETTIE *puts her arms around* JULIE
to comfort her. The GIRLS *group around them.*)

GIRLS

Common sense may tell you
That the endin' will be sad
And now's the time to break and run away,
But what's the use of wond'rin'
If the endin' will be sad?
He's your feller and you love him—
There's nothin' more to say.
(*The lights dim and the curtains close.*)

Scene 2

SCENE: *Mainland Waterfront. An hour later.*
*Extreme left there is an upright pile, a box, and a bale. At center
is a longer bale. Up right center is an assorted heap consisting of a
crate, a trunk, a sack, and other wharfside oddments.*

AT RISE: JIGGER *is seated on the pile extreme left, smoking.* BILLY *is
pacing back and forth, right center.*

BILLY

Suppose he don't come.

JIGGER

He'll come. What will you say to him?

BILLY

I say: "Good evening, sir. Excuse me, sir. Can you tell me the
time?" And suppose he answers me. What do I say?

JIGGER

He won't answer you.
    (JIGGER *throws his knife into the top of the box so that the
    point sticks and the knife quivers there.*)

BILLY

Have you ever—killed a man before?

JIGGER

If I did, I wouldn't be likely to say so, would I?

BILLY

No, guess you wouldn't. If you did—if tonight *we*—I mean—

suppose some day when we die we'll have to come up before—
before—

JIGGER

Before who?

BILLY

Well—before God.

JIGGER

You and me? Not a chance!

BILLY

Why not?

JIGGER

What's the highest court they ever dragged you into?

BILLY

Just perlice magistrates, I guess.

JIGGER

Sure. Never been before a supreme-court judge, have you?

BILLY

No.

JIGGER

Same thing in the next world. For rich folks, the heavenly court
and the high judge. For you and me, perlice magistrates. For the
rich, fine music and chubby little angels—

BILLY

Won't we get any music?

JIGGER

Not a note. All we'll get is justice! There'll be plenty of that for you and me. Yes, sir! Nothin' but justice.

BILLY

It's getting' late—they'll be comin' back from the clambake. I wish he'd come.—Suppose he don't.

JIGGER

He will. What do you say we play some cards while we're waitin'? Time'll pass quicker that way.

BILLY

All right.

JIGGER

Got any money?

BILLY

Eighty cents.
(*Crosses to* JIGGER, *sits on small bale, and puts his money on table.* JIGGER *takes out cards and his change.*)

JIGGER
(*Puts money on box top, shuffles cards*)
All right, eighty cents. We'll play twenty-one. I'll bank.
(*Deals the necessary cards out.*)

BILLY
(*Looking at his cards*)
I'll bet the bank.

JIGGER
(*Aloud, to himself*)
Sounds like he's got an ace.

BILLY
I'll take another. (JIGGER *deals another card to* BILLY) Come again!
(JIGGER *deals a fourth card*) Over! (*Throws cards down.* JIGGER
gathers in the money. BILLY *rises, crosses right center, looks off right*)
Wish old sideburns would come and have it over with.

JIGGER
He's a little late. (*Looking up at* BILLY) Don't you want to go on
with the game?

BILLY
Ain't got any more money. I told you.

JIGGER
Want to play on credit?

BILLY
You mean you'll trust me?

JIGGER
No—but I'll deduct it.

BILLY
From what?

JIGGER

From your share of the money. If you win, you deduct it from
my share.

BILLY
(*Crossing and sitting on bale*)
All right. Can't wait here doin' nothin'. Drive a feller crazy. How
much is the bank?

JIGGER

Sideburns'll have three thousand on him. That's what he always
brings the captain. Tonight the captain don't get it. We get it.
Fifteen hundred to you. Fifteen hundred to me.

BILLY

Go ahead and deal. (JIGGER *deals*) Fifty dollars. (*Looks at his card*)
No, a hundred dollars. (JIGGER *gives him a card*) Enough.

JIGGER
(*Laying down stack and looking at his own cards*)
Twenty-one.

BILLY

All right. This time double or nothin'!

JIGGER
(*Dealing*)
Double or nothin' it is.

BILLY
(*Looking at cards*)
Enough.

JIGGER

(*Laying down his cards*)

Twenty-one.

BILLY

Hey—are you cheatin'?

JIGGER

(*So innocent*)

Me? Do I look like a cheat?

BILLY

(BILLY *raps the box impatiently.* JIGGER *deals*)

Five hundred!

JIGGER

Dollars?

BILLY

Dollars.

JIGGER

Say, you're a plunger, ain't you? Yes, sir.

BILLY

(*Getting a card*)

Another. (*He gets it*) Too much.

JIGGER

That makes seven hundred you owe me.

BILLY

Seven hundred! Double or nothin'. (JIGGER *deals*) I'll stand pat!

JIGGER
(*Laying own his cards in pretended amazement*)
Twenty-one! A natural!

BILLY
(*Rising and taking hold of* JIGGER *by the coat lapels*)
You—you—damn you, you're a dirty crook! You—(BASCOMBE
enters from left. JIGGER *coughs, warning* BILLY, *and then nudges*
BILLY *into action as* BASCOMBE *crosses to right center.* JIGGER *runs*
behind crates. BILLY *addresses* BASCOMBE) Excuse me, sir. Can you
tell me the time?
(BASCOMBE *turns to* BILLY, *and* JIGGER *leaps out from behind*
the crates and tries to stab BASCOMBE. BASCOMBE *gets hold of*
JIGGER'*s knife hand and twists his wrist, forcing him into a*
helpless position. BASCOMBE *takes his gun from its holster*
with his free hand, holding BILLY *off.*)

BASCOMBE
Now don't budge, either one of you. (*To* JIGGER) Drop that
knife. (JIGGER *drops the knife*) Ahoy up there on the Nancy B!
Captain Watson! Anybody up there?

CAPTAIN
(*Off*)
Ahoy, down there!
(JIGGER *twists himself loose and runs off right. A* SAILOR *enters*
from left. BASCOMBE *turns and fires a shot at* JIGGER *as he runs,*
then turns, holding BILLY *off, as the sailor gets to* BASCOMBE.)

BASCOMBE
(*To the* SAILOR)
Go after that one. He's runnin' up Maple Street. I'll cover the
other one. (*The sailor runs off after* JIGGER) There's another bullet

in here. Don't forget that—you. Look behind you! What do you
see comin'?

BILLY
(*Slowly turning and looking off left*)
Two perlicemen.

BASCOMBE
You wanted to know what time it was. I'll tell you—the time for
you will be ten or twenty years in prison.
(*The* TWO POLICEMEN *enter from left.*)

BILLY
Oh, no it won't.
(*He clambers up on the pile with his knife drawn.*)

BASCOMBE
(*Jeering and covering him with his pistol*)
Where do you think you're escapin' to—the sky?

BILLY
They won't put me in no prison.
(*He raises the knife high in air.*)

POLICEMAN
Stop him!

BILLY
(*Stabbing himself in the stomach*)
Julie!
(*He topples off the pile of crates, falling behind them. The*
TWO POLICEMEN, *who have made a vain attempt to stop him,
rush behind the crates, where they proceed to remove his coat,*

which is later to be used for his pillow. The CAPTAIN *and* ANOTHER SAILOR *come on the run from left. The* CAPTAIN *is carrying a lantern, which he puts on the pile, right center.*)

CAPTAIN
(*To* BASCOMBE)
How about you, Mr. Bascombe? You all right?

BASCOMBE
Yes, I'm all right. Lucky, though. Very lucky. This is the first time I ever took a pistol with me.

CAPTAIN
(*Looking over crates at* BILLY)
Is he dead?

1ST POLICEMAN
I don't think so, he's still breathing.

CAPTAIN
Bring him out here where we can lay him out flat. (*The* CAPTAIN *looks around to see what can be used for a bed for* BILLY. *He spots the bales, crosses to left, takes the small bale, and puts it end to end with a larger one. The* TWO POLICEMEN *and the* SAILOR *carry* BILLY *out and lay him on the bales. The* CAPTAIN *speaks to the* SAILOR:) You go for a doctor. (*To the* POLICEMAN *who is holding* BILLY'*s coat*) Put that under his head.
    (*The policeman does this. When* BILLY *is set, the* TWO POLICE-MEN *rise; one stands left end of bale, the other right end.*)

BASCOMBE
The fools—the silly fools. They didn't even notice I was comin' from the ship, not to it.

(*The* CAPTAIN *is covering* BILLY *with a tarpaulin he found on the top of crates at right center.*)

CAPTAIN

The money they tried to kill you for is locked up in my desk! (*Voices off left are heard to be singing "June Is Bustin' Out All Over," very softly, as if in the distance.*)

BASCOMBE

The fools.

1ST SAILOR
(*The one who chased* JIGGER, *returning*)

He got away.

BASCOMBE
(*Hearing the offstage singing as it has become louder*)

What's that?

CAPTAIN

The folks comin' back from the clambake.
(*The people enter left.*)

BASCOMBE
(*To the* POLICEMAN)

You'd better stop them.
(BASCOMBE *exits.*)

POLICEMAN

Yes, sir. (*They cross over and stop the crowd from reaching* BILLY, *but one or two get through and see the tragedy, and they recognize*

BILLY. *The* POLICEMEN *get to these and speak. The singing stops)* Get back there. Stand back.

(A voice is heard from behind the crowd.)

1ST VOICE

Who is it?

2ND VOICE

Billy.

3RD VOICE

Billy Bigelow.

4TH VOICE

Poor Julie.

(The crowd opens up for JULIE, *who goes straight to* BILLY, *up behind the bales.* NETTIE *and the* POLICEMEN *hurry the crowd off quietly. They exit left. The* CAPTAIN *remains on right of the crates looking upstage. The* POLICEMEN *and* NETTIE *also remain.)*

JULIE
(As she is crossing to him)

Billy—

BILLY

Little Julie—somethin' I want to tell you—(*Pause*) I couldn't see anythin' ahead, and Jigger told me how we could get a hold of a lot of money—and maybe sail to San Francisco.—See?

JULIE

Yes.

BILLY

Tell the baby, if you want, say I had this idea about San Francisco. (*His voice grows weaker*) Julie—

JULIE

Yes.

BILLY

Hold my hand tight.

JULIE

I am holdin' it tight—all the time.

BILLY

Tighter—still tighter! (*Pause*) Julie!

JULIE

Good-by.
　(*He sinks back.* JULIE *kisses his hand. The* CAPTAIN *crosses
　over, picks* JULIE *up gently. He then bends down and inspects*
　BILLY. *He rises, looks at* JULIE.)

CAPTAIN

The good lord will help him now, ma'am.
　(CARRIE *enters, followed by* SNOW. *They cross to* JULIE's *left.*)

CARRIE

Julie—don't be mad at me fer sayin' it—but you're better off
this way.

SNOW

Carrie's right.

CARRIE

Julie, tell me, am I right?

JULIE

You're right, Carrie.

CARRIE
(*Looking down at* BILLY)
He's better off too, poor feller. Believe me, Julie, he's better off
too.
(*She embraces* JULIE, *weeping.*)

JULIE

Don't cry, Carrie.

CARRIE

God be with you, Julie.
(JULIE *smiles at her wearily.* SNOW *takes* CARRIE *by the arm
and leads her off down left. We hear voices off left.*)

MRS. MULLIN
(*Off left*)
Where is he? No, no please.
(MRS. MULLIN *comes in on the run from left, followed by
TWO GIRLS, who try to stop her.*)

GIRL

Don't let her!
(MRS. MULLIN *stops left center, looks at* BILLY, *then at* JULIE
questioningly. JULIE *steps back—a silent invitation to come
and pass in front of her.* MRS. MULLIN *walks slowly to where
BILLY lies. After a moment she brushes* BILLY's *hair off his
forehead, as she used to do. Then* NETTIE, *the* POLICEMAN

and all exit, leaving only JULIE *and* MRS. MULLIN *on the stage with* BILLY. MRS. MULLIN *gets up and turns slowly to look at* JULIE, *who looks back at her.* MRS. MULLIN *tries a faint little smile, then turns and exits left.* JULIE *returns to* BILLY, *leans over, and restores the stray lock to where it was before* MRS. MULLIN *took the liberty to brush it back.*)

JULIE

Sleep, Billy—sleep. Sleep peaceful, like a good boy. I knew why you hit me. You were quick-tempered and unhappy. I always knew everythin' you were thinkin'. But you didn't always know what I was thinkin'. One thing I never told you—skeered you'd laugh at me. I'll tell you now—(*Even now she has to make an effort to overcome her shyness in saying it*) I love you. I love you. (*In a whisper*) I love—you. (*Smiles*) I was always ashamed to say it out loud. But now I said it. Didn't I? (*She takes the shawl off her shoulders and drapes it over* BILLY. NETTIE *comes in from left.* JULIE *looks up and sees her, lets out a cry, and runs to her*) What am I goin' to do?

NETTIE

Do? Why, you gotta stay on here with me—so's I ken be with you when you hev the baby. (JULIE *buries her head in* NETTIE*'s shoulder and holds tightly to her*) Main thing is to keep on livin'— keep on *keerin'* what's goin' to happen. 'Member that sampler you gave me? 'Member what it says?

JULIE

The words? Sure. Used to sing 'em in school.

NETTIE

Sing 'em now—see if you know what they mean.

JULIE
(*Singing*)

When you walk
Through a storm
Keep your chin up high,
And don't be afraid—of—the—dar—
(JULIE *breaks off, sobbing.* NETTIE *starts the song.*)

NETTIE
(*Singing*)

When you walk
Through a storm
Keep your chin up high,
And don't be afraid of the dark.
At the end
Of the storm
Is a golden sky
And the sweet
Silver song
Of a lark.

Walk on
Through the wind,
Walk on
Through the rain,
Though your dreams be tossed and blown,
Walk on, walk on,
With hope in your heart,
And you'll never walk alone!
You'll never walk alone.
(JULIE *and* NETTIE *kneel in prayer. The* TWO HEAVENLY
FRIENDS *enter from right and cross to* BILLY.)

1ST HEAVENLY FRIEND

Get up, Billy.

BILLY

Huh?

1ST HEAVENLY FRIEND

Get up.

BILLY
(*Straightening up*)

Who are you?

2ND HEAVENLY FRIEND

Shake yourself up. Got to get goin'.

BILLY
(*Looking up at them and turning front, still sitting*)

Goin'? Where?

1ST HEAVENLY FRIEND

Never mind where. Important thing is you can't stay here.

BILLY
(*Turning left, looks at* JULIE)

Julie!

(*The lights dim, and a cloud gauze drop comes in behind* BILLY *and the* HEAVENLY FRIENDS.)

1ST HEAVENLY FRIEND

She can't hear you.

BILLY

Who decided that?

1ST HEAVENLY FRIEND

You did. When you killed yourself.

BILLY

I see! So it's over!

1ST HEAVENLY FRIEND

It isn't as simple as that. As long as there is one person on earth who remembers you—it isn't over.

BILLY

What're you goin' to do to me?

1ST HEAVENLY FRIEND

We aren't going to do anything. We jest came down to fetch you—take you up to the jedge.

BILLY

Judge! Am I goin' before the Lord God Himself?

1ST HEAVENLY FRIEND

What hev you ever done thet you should come before Him?

BILLY
(*His anger rising*)

So that's it. Just like Jigger said; "No supreme court for little people—jest perlice magistrates"!

1ST HEAVENLY FRIEND

Who said anythin' about—

BILLY

I tell you if they kick me around up there like they did on earth,
I'm goin' to do somethin' about it! I'm dead and I got nothin' to
lose. I'm goin' to stand up for my rights! I tell you I'm goin' before
the Lord God Himself—straight to the top! Y'hear?

1ST HEAVENLY FRIEND

Simmer down, Billy.

BILLY

(*Singing*)

Take me beyond the pearly gates
Through a beautiful marble hall,
Take me before the highest throne
And let me judged by the highest Judge of all!

Let the Lord shout and yell,
Let His eyes flash flame,
I promise not to quiver when He calls my name,
Let Him send me to hell,
But before I go,
I feel that I'm entitled to a hell of a show!
Want pink-faced angels on a purple cloud,
Twangin' on their harps till their fingers get red,
Want organ music—let it roll out loud,
Rollin' like a wave, washin' over my head!
Want ev'ry star in heaven
Hangin' in the room,
Shinin' in my eyes
When I hear my doom!

Reckon my sins are good big sins,
And the punishment won't be small;

So take me before the highest throne
And let me be judged by the highest Judge of all.
　　(1ST HEAVENLY FRIEND *gestures to* BILLY *to follow. They exit.*)

Scene 3

SCENE: *Up there.*

A celestial clothes-line is seen stretching back through infinity, but one portion of it is strung across as far downstage as possible. There is a celestial stepladder standing right center upstage of the line. It resembles our own stepladders except that it shimmers with a silvery light. The clothes-line is quite full of shimmering stars. There is a basket full of stars on the shelf behind the ladder.

AT RISE: *The* STARKEEPER *is seated on the top of the stepladder, and as the lights come up, he can be seen hanging out stars and dusting them with a silver-handled white feather duster.*

BILLY *and the* TWO HEAVENLY FRIENDS *are seen making their way through the clouds from stage left to right, emerging a moment later through entrance down right into the back yard. The* 1ST HEAVENLY FRIEND *enters. He stops, stage right center, faces front, and speaks.*

1ST HEAVENLY FRIEND

Billy!

BILLY
(Entering)

Hey what is this! (*Crossing and speaking to* STARKEEPER) Who are you?

STARKEEPER

Never mind who I am, Bigelow.

BILLY
(To FRIEND)

Where am I?

STARKEEPER
(*Although question was not addressed to him*)
You're in the back yard of heaven. (*Pointing off right*) There's the gates over there.

BILLY
The pearly gates!

STARKEEPER
Nope. The pearly gates are in front. Those are the back gates. They're just mother-of-pearly.

BILLY
I don't wanta go in no back gate. I wanta go before the highest—

STARKEEPER
You'll go where we send you, young man.

BILLY
Now look here!

STARKEEPER
Don't yell.

BILLY
I didn't yell.

STARKEEPER
Well, don't. (*He takes a star off the line. To* FRIEND) This one's finished. Brother Joshua, please hang it over Salem, Mass.

1ST HEAVENLY FRIEND
(*Crossing over and taking star*)

A-ya.

(*Exits off left.*)

STARKEEPER
(*Taking a notebook out of his pocket*)
Now, this is a routine question I gotta ask everybody. Is there anythin' on earth you left unfinished? The reason I ask you is you're entitled to go back fer one day—if you want to.

BILLY
I don't know. (*Doggedly*) Guess as long as I'm here, I won't go back.

STARKEEPER
(*Jotting down in a notebook*)
"Waives his right to go back."

BILLY
Can I ask you somethin'? I'd like to know if the baby will be a boy or a girl.

STARKEEPER
We'll come to that later.

BILLY
But I'm only askin'—

STARKEEPER
Jest let me do the askin'—you do the answerin'. I got my orders.— You left yer wife hevin' thet baby comin'—with nothin' fer 'em to live on. Why'd you do thet?

BILLY

I couldn't get work and I couldn't bear to see her—
(*Pause.*)

STARKEEPER

You couldn't bear to see her cry. Why not come right out and
say it? Why are you afraid of sayin' the right word? Why are you
ashamed you loved Julie?

BILLY

I ain't ashamed of anything.

STARKEEPER

Why'd you beat her?

BILLY

I didn't beat her—I wouldn't beat a little thing like that—I hit
her.

STARKEEPER

Why?

BILLY

Well, y'see—we'd argue. And she'd say this and I'd say that—
and she'd be right—so I'd hit her.

STARKEEPER

Hmm! Are you sorry you hit her?

BILLY

Ain't sorry fer anthin'.

STARKEEPER
(*Taking his basket and coming down off the ladder*)
You ken be as sot and pernicketty as you want. Up here patience
is as endless as time. We ken wait. (*He turns to* BILLY *in a more
friendly way*) Now look here, son, it's only fair to tell you—
you're in a pretty tight corner. Fact is you haven't done enough
good in yer life to get in there—not even through the back door.

BILLY
(*Turning away*)
All right. If I can't get in—I can't.

STARKEEPER
(*Testily*)
I didn't say you can't. Said you ain't done enough so *far*. You
might still make it—if you tried hard enough.

BILLY
How?

STARKEEPER
Why don't you go down to earth fer a day like I said you could.
Do somethin' real fine fer someone.

BILLY
Aw—what could I do?

STARKEEPER
Well, fer one thing you might do yer little daughter some good.

BILLY
(*Turning to* STARKEEPER, *elated*)
A daughter! It's a girl—my baby!

STARKEEPER

Ain't a baby any more. She's fifteen years old.

BILLY

How could that be? I just come from there.

STARKEEPER

You got to get used to a new way of tellin' time, Billy. A year on earth is just a minute up here. Would you like to look down and see her?

BILLY

Could I? Could I see her from here?

STARKEEPER

Sure could. Follow me.
   (STARKEEPER *and* BILLY *cross down right. The lights dim and the gauze cloud curtain descends behind them.*)

BILLY

Tell me—is she happy?

STARKEEPER

No, she ain't, Billy. She's a lot like you. That's why I figure you're the one could help her most—if you was there.

BILLY

If she ain't happy, I don't want to look.

STARKEEPER

(*Looking off left, as if toward the earth*)
Well, right this minute she appears to be hevin' a fine time. Yes, sir! There she is, runnin' on the beach. Got her shoes and stockin's off.

BILLY

Like I used to do!

STARKEEPER

Don't you think you better take a look?

BILLY

Where is she? What do I have to do to see her?

STARKEEPER

Jest look and wait. The power to see her will come to you.
(*He puts his hand lightly on* BILLY'*s shoulder.*)

BILLY

Is that her? Little kid with straw-colored hair?
(*The lights dim. The curtain goes up on a dark stage.*)

STARKEEPER
(*As the lights are dimming*)

Pretty—ain't she?

BILLY

My little girl!
(BILLY *and the* STARKEEPER *back off down right and the entire
stage is suddenly flooded with light.*)

Scene 4

SCENE: *Down here. On a beach. Fifteen years later.*

Ballet

AT RISE: LOUISE *is romping on the beach. Two little* RUFFIAN BOYS *join her. Presently* ENOCH SNOW *enters, leading his six very well-behaved* CHILDREN. LOUISE *invites them to join in her play, but, taking their cue from their father's horrified face, they snub her. They exit with their father, all except one little horror in a big hat who remains to taunt* LOUISE.

SNOW'S DAUGHTER
My father bought me my pretty dress.

LOUISE
My father would have bought me a pretty dress, too. He was a barker on a carousel.

SNOW'S DAUGHTER
Your father was a thief.
(Her nasty work accomplished, she assumes an impish, satisfied look and starts away. LOUISE *goes after her. Their pace increases.* LOUISE *finally chasing her off, returning soon with a trophy— the big hat.*

(Now a CARNIVAL TROUPE *dances on. The* RUFFIANS *are frightened by them. Failing to persuade* LOUISE *to run away with them, they leave her there. One of the carnival boys is the type* LOUISE'S *father was when he was young. Of all this fascinating group, he interests her most. After the others dance off, he returns to her for a flirtation. It is much more than this to* LOUISE. *It is a first experience, overwhelmingly beautiful,*

painful and passionate. He leaves her abruptly. She's too young.
Thwarted, humiliated, she weeps alone.

(*Now a group of* CHILDREN *enter, dressed for a part.* LOUISE
seeks consolation with them. She tries to join in their dancing.
They reject her and make fun of her. She turns on them so
viciously that they are frozen with awe and fear as she speaks
to them in a voice full of deep injury and the fury of a hopeless
outcast.)

                              LOUISE
I hate you—I hate all of you!
(*They back away, then dance away, leaving her heartbroken*
and alone—terribly alone.)

(*The gauze cloud curtain falls, revealing* BILLY *and the* STAR-
KEEPER, *who have been watching all this from "up there."*)

                              BILLY
Why did you make me look?

                            STARKEEPER
You said you wanted to.

                              BILLY
I know what she's goin' through.

                            STARKEEPER
Somethin' like what happened to you when you was a kid, ain't it?

                              BILLY
Somebody ought to help her.

STARKEEPER

Ay-ah. Somebody ought to. You ken go down any time. Offer's still open.

(*The* 1ST HEAVENLY FRIEND *enters to guide* BILLY *if he wants to go.* BILLY *starts toward him; then, getting a sudden idea, he turns back and stealthily takes a star from the* STARKEEPER'S *basket. Both the* STARKEEPER *and the* HEAVENLY FRIEND *are aware of this, but pretend not to notice.* BILLY *waves an elaborate good-by to the* STARKEEPER *and, whistling casually to quell suspicion, he starts away with the* HEAVENLY FRIEND.)

Scene 5

SCENE: *Outside Julie's cottage.*

AT RISE: JULIE *and* CARRIE *are seated outside the cottage, having coffee.*

CARRIE
(*Seated, left of* JULIE, *continuing a narrative*)
—and so the next day we all climbed to the top of the Statue of Liberty—Enoch and me and the nine kids.

JULIE
Did you go to any theayters in New York?

CARRIE
'Course we did!

JULIE
Did you see any of them there "extravaganzas"?

CARRIE
Enoch took me to one of them things. The curtain went up and the fust thing y'see is twelve hussies and nothin' on their legs but tights!

JULIE
What happened then?

CARRIE
Well! Enoch jest grabbed hold o' my arm and dragged me out of the theayter! But I went back the next day—to a matinee—to see how the story come out.

JULIE

All by yerself? (CARRIE *nods*) Lucky you didn't see anybody you know.

CARRIE

I did.

JULIE

Who?

CARRIE

Enoch!
    (JULIE *claps her hand over her mouth to keep from laughing.
    Then she gets the cups together.* CARRIE *gets up.*)

CARRIE
(*Animatedly*)

There was one girl who sung an awful ketchy song. (*She walks to the back of her chair.* LOUISE *enters from the house, unnoticed*) she threw her leg over a fence like this—(*As she is swinging her leg over the chair, she sees* LOUISE *and hastily puts her leg down*)—and it rained all day!
    (JULIE, *her back toward* LOUISE, *stares at* CARRIE *in wonder.
    She gathers that something is up, turns right, and sees* LOUISE.)

JULIE

Oh-h-h. Louise, take these cups right into the kitchen, dear. That's a good girl.
    (LOUISE *takes the cups into the house.*)

CARRIE

She threw her leg over a fence like this—(*She swings her leg over the chair and pulls her skirt up over her knee*) and she sung:

(*She sings:*)
I'm a tomboy,
Jest a tomboy!
I'm a madcap maiden from Broadway!
  (ENOCH *enters, followed by their* ELDEST SON, *but* CARRIE
  does not see them. JULIE *tries to warn her*)
I'm a tomboy,
A merry tomboy!

ENOCH
(*Taking his son by the shoulders*)
Turn yer eyes away, Junior!
(*Turns his son's face away.*)

CARRIE
(*Taking her leg off the chair and standing there guiltily*)
I was jest tellin' Julie about thet show—*Madcap Maidens.*

ENOCH
We also saw *Julius Cæsar.* Wouldn't thet be a better play to quote
from?

CARRIE
I don't remember much of thet one. All the men was dressed in
nightgowns and it made me sleepy.

JULIE
(*Trying to change the subject*)
Won't you set down and visit with us?

ENOCH
Afeared we hevn't time. Mrs. Snow and I hev to stop at the

minister's on our way to the graduation. (*To* CARRIE) And I'll thank you not to sing "I'm a tomboy" to the minister's wife.

CARRIE

I already did.

ENOCH

(*Giving his son a good slap on the back with his right hand*)
Come, Junior!
(LOUISE *comes out of the house just as* JUNIOR *turns to his father.* JUNIOR *sees* LOUISE *and gets a new idea.*)

ENOCH, JR.

Pa, ken I stay and talk to Louise? (ENOCH *looks stern.* CARRIE *crosses to* ENOCH) Jest fer five minutes.

ENOCH

No!

CARRIE

(*Slapping* ENOCH's *back in the same manner as*
ENOCH *slapped* JUNIOR)
Aw, let him!

ENOCH

All right. Five minutes. No more.

JULIE

(*Going into house*)
Good-by.

CARRIE
See you at the graduation.
(JULIE *exits into house.*)

ENOCH
(*Taking* CARRIE *to exit*)
Still lallygaggin'. You'd think a woman with nine children'd have
more sense.

CARRIE
If I hed more sense I wouldn't hev nine children!
(*She crosses in front of* ENOCH *and exits. He follows.*)

LOUISE
I wish I could go to New York.

ENOCH, JR.
What are you goin' to do after you graduate?

LOUISE
(*Lowering her voice, as* BILLY *and* FRIEND *enter left*)
Listen, Enoch—ken you keep a secret?
(JUNIOR *solemnly crosses his heart and spits.*)

BILLY
(*To* HEAVENLY FRIEND)
Can she see me?

1ST HEAVENLY FRIEND
Only if you want her to.
(*They remain silent observers of the scene,* BILLY *standing by
the trellis,* HEAVENLY FRIEND *extreme downstage left.*)

ENOCH, JR.

Well, what's the secret?

LOUISE

I'm goin' to be an actress. There's a troupe comin' through here next week. I met a feller—says he's the advance man, or somethin'—says he'll help me.

ENOCH, JR.
(*Horrified*)

You mean run away? (*She puts her fingers to her lips to shush him.* BILLY *winces.* 1ST HEAVENLY FRIEND *watches* BILLY) I won't let you do it, Louise.

LOUISE

How'll you stop me?

ENOCH, JR.

I'll marry you. That's how. The hardest thing'll be to persuade Papa to let me marry beneath my station.

LOUISE

You needn't bother about marryin' beneath your station! I wouldn't have you. And I wouldn't have that stuck-up buzzard for a father-in-law if you give me a million dollars!
(BILLY *looks at* FRIEND *and smiles, happy over this.*)

ENOCH, JR.
(*Outraged, hit in a tender spot*)

You're a fine one to talk about my father! What about yer own? A cheap barker on a carousel—and he beat your mother!

LOUISE

(*Giving* JUNIOR *a good punch*)
You get out of here! You sleeky little la-de-da! (*Spins him around, gives him a well-directed kick.* BILLY, *seeing all this, puts out his foot and trips* JUNIOR *just as he is passing him*) I'll—I'll kill you—you—
(JUNIOR *runs off left.* LOUISE *suddenly turns, crosses to her chair, sinks on it, and sobs.* BILLY *looks over at* LOUISE, *who is a very heartbroken little girl. He turns to the* HEAVENLY FRIEND.)

BILLY

If I want her to see me, she will? (*The* HEAVENLY FRIEND *nods.* BILLY *approaches* LOUISE *timidly*) Little girl—Louise!
(*She looks up through her tears.*)

LOUISE

Who are you?

BILLY

I—I—
(*He's nearly as rattled as he was the night he suddenly faced* BASCOMBE *on the wharf.*)

LOUISE

How did you know my name?

BILLY

Somebody told me you lived here. I knew your father.

LOUISE

My father!

BILLY

I heard what that little whippersnapper said. It ain't true—any
of it.

LOUISE

It is true—all of it.
(*Pause. He is stunned.*)

BILLY

Did your mother tell you that?

LOUISE

No, but every kid in town knows it. They've been throwin' it up
at me ever since I kin remember. I wish I was dead.
(*She looks away to hide her tears.*)

BILLY
(*Softly*)
What—what did yer *mother* say about—him?

LOUISE

Oh, she's told me a lot of fairy stories about how he died in San
Francisco—and she's always sayin' what a handsome fellow he
was—

BILLY

Well, he was!

LOUISE
(*Hopefully, rising*)
Was he—really?

BILLY

He was the handsomest feller around here.

LOUISE

You really knew him, did you? And he was handsome. (*He nods his head*) What else about him? Know anythin' else *good* about him?

BILLY
(*Passing right hand through his hair*)
Well-ll—he used to tell funny jokes at the carousel and make people laugh.

LOUISE
(*Her face lighting up*)
Did he? (*They both laugh*) What else?
(*Pause. He's stuck and changes the subject.*)

BILLY

Look—I want to give you a present.

LOUISE
(*Backing up right, immediately suspicious*)
Don't come in, mister, my mother wouldn't like it.

BILLY

I don't mean you any harm, child. I want to give you somethin'.

LOUISE

Don't you come any closer. You go 'way with yer white face. You scare me.

BILLY

Don't chase me away. I want to give you a present—somethin' pretty—somethin' wonderful.

(*He looks at* HEAVENLY FRIEND, *who turns front and smiles.* BILLY *takes the star from his inside vest pocket.* LOUISE *looks at star, then at* BILLY.)

LOUISE

What's that?

BILLY

Pst! A star.

(*He points up to the sky with right hand to indicate whence it came.* LOUISE *is terrified now.*)

LOUISE
(*Backing up right*)

Go away!

BILLY
(*Growing panicky and taking her arm*)

Darling, please—I want to help you.

LOUISE
(*Trying to pull arm away*)

Don't call me darling. Let go my arm!

BILLY

I want to make you happy. Take this—

LOUISE

No!

BILLY

Please! (*She pulls away from him, holding out her right hand to keep him away from her*) Please—dear—
(*Impulsively, involuntarily, he slaps her hand. She is startled.*)

LOUISE

Mother! (*She runs into the house*) Mother!
(BILLY *puts star on the chair nearest center. Then he looks at* FRIEND *guiltily.*)

1ST HEAVENLY FRIEND

Failure! You struck out blindly again. All you ever do to get out of a difficulty—hit someone you love! Failure!

JULIE
(*Coming out of house, agitated*)

Where is he?
(*She stops suddenly.* BILLY *turns to her. She stares at him.*)

BILLY
(*To* HEAVENLY FRIEND, *but looking at* JULIE)

I don't want her to see me.

1ST HEAVENLY FRIEND

Then she doesn't.

BILLY

She looks like she saw me before I said that.

LOUISE
(*Coming out of the house and crossing downstage
of* BILLY, *almost touching him*)

Oh, he's gone! (*Turning to* JULIE) I didn't make it up, Mother.

Honest there was a strange man here and he hit me—hard—I
heard the sound of it—but it didn't hurt, Mother! It didn't hurt
at all—it was jest as if he—kissed my hand!

JULIE

Go into the house, child.

LOUISE

What's happened, Mother? (JULIE *just stares at the same place*)
Don't you believe me?

JULIE

Yes, I believe you.

LOUISE
(*Coming closer to* JULIE)
Then why don't you tell me why you're actin' so funny?

JULIE

It's nothin', darlin'.

LOUISE

But is it possible, Mother, fer someone to hit you hard like
that—real loud and hard—and not hurt you at all?

JULIE

It is possible, dear—fer someone to hit you—hit you hard—
and not hurt at all.
(JULIE *and* LOUISE *embrace and start for the house.* LOUISE
exits into house, but JULIE *sees the star that* BILLY *had placed
on the chair and goes toward it. As she does so, the lights dim
slowly. She picks up the star and holds it to her breast.*)

BILLY

Julie—Julie!

(*She stands transfixed. He sings:*)
Longing to tell you,
But afraid and shy,
I let my golden chances pass me by
Now I've lost you;
Soon I will go in the mist of day,
And you never will know
How I loved you,
How I loved you.

(*The lights fade out as* JULIE *goes into the house. As* BILLY *crosses to the* HEAVENLY FRIEND, *the cloud curtain falls behind him*)
She took the star—she took it! Seems like she knew I was here.

1ST HEAVENLY FRIEND

Julie would always know.

BILLY

She never changes.

1ST HEAVENLY FRIEND

No, Julie never changes.

BILLY

But my little girl—my Louise—I gotta do somethin' fer her.

1ST HEAVENLY FRIEND

So far you haven't done much.

BILLY

I know. I know.

1ST HEAVENLY FRIEND

Time's running out.

BILLY

But it ain't over yet. I want an extension! I gotta see her graduation.

1ST HEAVENLY FRIEND

All right, Billy.
(*They exit. The blue lights dim on the curtain. The curtain rises in the dark. The lights flash up on the next scene*)

Scene 6

SCENE: *Outside a schoolhouse. Same day.*

AT RISE: *The graduating class sits massed on three rows of benches. The* GIRLS, *all dressed alike in white, are seated on the first two benches. The* BOYS, *wearing blue serge suits, sit on the third bench. The boys who cannot be seated on the third bench are standing on the steps of the schoolhouse, behind the benches. Stage left is a bench standing at an angle.* JULIE *is seated on the downstage end of this bench,* NETTIE *is seated alongside of her. There are two other persons on this bench and other relatives of the graduating class are lined up behind it. Stage right, there is a small platform on which is a speakers' stand. Upstage of this stand,* DR. SELDON *is seated on a chair.* MR. BASCOMBE *is seated on a chair downstage of the stand.* MR. AND MRS. SNOW *and their entire family are standing downstage right.* LOUISE *is seated on the extreme left end of the first bench with the graduating girls.*

As the lights come up, the PRINCIPAL *is standing behind the speakers' stand. All are applauding and a young* GIRL *has just received her diploma. She goes up and joins the others.*

PRINCIPAL

Enoch Snow, Junior!
> (ENOCH, JR., *comes up. His applause is led by his not inconsiderable family—*ENOCH, SR., CARRIE, *and his* BROTHERS *and* SISTERS. *They form a solid cheering section. As* ENOCH *returns to his place, one of the* GIRLS *sitting in the first row puts out her foot and trips him. He looks around, and she applauds vigorously. He walks on.*)

BABY SISTER

Yah!
> (CARRIE *pulls her back in line with rest of family.*)

PRINCIPAL

Miss Louise Bigelow. (JULIE *steps out and applauds.* CARRIE *claps her hands a few times, and there is not much more.* LOUISE *walks up, receives her diploma sullenly, and joins the group again.* BILLY *and the* HEAVENLY FRIEND *have come in, down right, in time to see this. The* PRINCIPAL *introduces the* DOCTOR) Our speaker this year is the most popular, best-loved man in our town—Dr. Seldon.

(*The* PRINCIPAL *steps down from the speakers' stand and stands behind* MR. BASCOMBE. DR. SELDON *now takes his place on the stand. He adjusts his spectacles, and as he does so,* BILLY *speaks to the* HEAVENLY FRIEND.)

BILLY

Say! He reminds me of that feller up on the ladder.

HEAVENLY FRIEND

Yes, a lot of these country doctors and ministers remind you of him.

DOCTOR

It's the custom at these graduations to pick out some old duck like me to preach at the kids. (*Laughter*) I can't preach at you. Know you all too well. Brought most of you into the world. Rubbed liniment on yer backs, poured castor oil down yer throats. (*A shudder runs through them, and a* GIRL *laughs. All look at her and she is mortified*) Well, all I hope is that now I got you this far, you'll turn out to be worth all the trouble I took with you! (*He pauses, looks steadily at them, his voice more earnest*) You can't lean on the successes of your parents. That's their success. (*Directing his words to* LOUISE) And don't be held back by their failures! Makes no difference what they did or didn't do. You jest stand on yer own two feet.

BILLY
(*To* LOUISE)
Listen to him. Believe him.
(*She looks up suddenly.*)

DOCTOR
The world belongs to you as much as to the next feller. Don't
give it up! And try not to be skeered o' people not likin' you—
jest you try likin' *them.* Jest keep yer faith and courage and you'll
come out all right. It's like what we used to sing every mornin'
when I went to school. Mebbe you still sing it—I dunno.
(*He recites*)
"When you walk through a storm,
Keep yer chin up high—"
(*To the kids*)
Know that one?
(*They nod eagerly and go on with the song.*)

ALL
And don't be afraid of the dark.

BILLY
(*To* LOUISE)
Believe him, darling! Believe.
(LOUISE *joins the others as they sing.*)

ALL
At the end of the storm
Is a golden sky
And the sweet silver song
Of a lark.
(BILLY *crosses back of bench left and stands behind* JULIE)
Walk on

Through the wind,
Walk on
Through the rain,
Though your dreams be tossed and blown.

BILLY
(To JULIE)
I loved you, Julie. Know that I loved you!
(JULIE's *face lights up and she starts singing with the rest.*)

ALL
Walk on,
Walk on,
With hope in your heart,
And you'll never walk alone.
    (LOUISE *moves in closer to the group. The* GIRL *to her right puts her arm around her. Her eyes shine. The* HEAVENLY FRIEND *smiles and beckons* BILLY *to follow him.* BILLY *does.*
    As they pass the DOCTOR, *he watches and smiles wisely*)
You'll never walk alone.

CURTAIN

PHOTOGRAPH CREDITS

Page numbers refer to the inserts.

Pages 1, 2, 3, 4, and 5: Courtesy of Rodgers & Hammerstein, An Imagem Company. www.rnh.com

Page 6: © Michael le Poer Trench

Pages 6, 7, and 8: © Joan Marcus

Pages 9 and 10: © Paul Kolnik

Page 11: From the respective papers of Richard Rodgers and Oscar Hammerstein II at the Library of Congress, Music Division, Washington, D.C.

Page 12: © Todd Rosenberg